Published by: *The Serengeti Network, a Division of Serengeti Entertainment*

582 Halsey Street
Brooklyn, New York 11233
**347-267-8083**

Copyright © 2016 by Lloyd Weaver and Ademola Fabunmi

All rights reserved. Reproduction of this book, or parts thereof, in any form without the written permission of the publisher is illegal and punishable by law.

ISBN: 978-0-692-79332-9

Editor: Karen Quinones-Miller

Cover Art: Gyimah Opare

First Print September 2016

Printed in the United States

# A BROOKLYN STREET CORNER 2010 – DAY,

Recently returned from thirty five years in Nigeria, Olorisa Lloyd Weaver (Baba Lloyd) recognizes a group of young initiates in the ancient Yoruba belief system often referred to as Lucumi or Ocha hanging on a Brooklyn street corner. They were in their eary teens when he left, but the memories are indelible; he is startled when they greet him with screams and hugs. Mindful of the changes in the socio/political milleu of African Americans (gentrification of the hood, mass encarceration scaling up, endemic joblessness, police terrorism and now Trump's exposure of the real underbelly of America) Baba Lloyd sees an opportunity to catch up and slides into the teaching/challenging mode with which he taught their parents.

> *"Okay people, so tell me....What is the path to truth, goodness, beauty, honor and evolution?"*

> *"Well dag Baba Lloyd, it's nice you back, we really missed you, but you been in Africa for thirty-three years now, how you gon come testin us? What you been learning over there? Why don't you tell us something we never knew?"*

Oh oh, things really have changed. These kids (Did I say kids?) have heared of African religion but have they heard of African *manners*? However, ahem, really, good question! In a world that is as competitive as ours, in which entire nations, and worse, entire races and ethnicities live in desperate hatred and fear of one another, where we remember 9/11 one day and police choke a man to death in a nearby neighborhood the next, one wonders if *sensible living* means carrying a gun, or at least a can of mace; where security and even survival are seen as the watchwords of sensible living? But despite it all, a world in which style and popularity can be more important than honor and character, where a movie isn't worth watching unless there is a good sex scene in the middle of it. Obviously, whatever I learned in Africa is going to sound pretty lame in Brooklyn. So let me try this:

> *"What if I tell you that in Africa I am often asked to lead ceremonies because the religious practices there are almost the same as what we do here except they sometimes recognize ours as older. Plus they think my broken Yoruba is funny. The main difference is that people's <u>values</u> are different. People here <u>talk about</u> Iwa Pele[1]. Over there few people talk about it but everybody tries to <u>live it</u>. You know, the way you carry yourself and what you do are more important than anything. And, oh yes, they don't call it "Iwa Pele," they usually call it "Iwa Rere"[2].*

> *"Hey Boo, whas he talkin about?"*

> *"Don't worry Chichi, I got this. (Turns back to me) Yeah Baba Lloyd, that's nice an all that but over here it's different, you have to be ready to take care of your self. We try to be happy, partying and everything, and we really down with the religion, but the preparedness to do what you have to do is a matter of life in the city, that's just the way it is. Right? So while you talking about Iwa Pele or Rere or whatever you want to call it, our <u>reality</u> is a little different."*

Do what you have to do? Take care of yourself? What *'reality?'*

> *"So then why do you want to know what I learned in Africa?"*
>
> *"Cause you Baba Lloyd; you know about Africa and you know about us. Ain't you got some funny Orisa[3] stories that can teach us something? Help us roll a little better, you know."*
>
> *"Stories? Oh, you want me to tell you stories I learned in Africa?*
>
> *"Yeah, right, but don't come with no riddles. This is still Brooklyn you know. Tell us what we don't know!"*
>
> *"Tell you something? Like what?"*
>
> *"Baba Lloyd, I don't mean no disrespect, but sometimes I don't know about you. We just want to know how to be happy. I'm a girl and this thing in my bag is too heavy to be carrying around, and besides, Ogun told me to put it in his pot...with palm oil all over the thing. So explain to me again what's with Ogun?"*

And so we wonder; as we continually grapple with the quintissential question: *what is the meaning of life?*, even we priests, supposed holy men and women, teachers of the Book, you know, even we sometimes wonder if it is moral to teach our children, you know, how to use that glock <u>you</u> have stashed in that box under the floor of that storage closet?

Okay, maybe that's a little crazy, but this was a conversation I had with a couple of young, 2nd generation Olorisa[4] while visiting *home* recently. But really I could have had it with almost anybody; I mean in many ways it applies to all of us.

"Really?" you ask. "A glock?"

And I'm saying Yes, <u>really</u> (and let's hope the police don't read this; they'll be raiding our homes to see what we have with Ogun!). I mean I talk to everybody. Times and circumstances are changing so fast that in our desperate search for answers to questions that really have no answers many of us find ourselves switching pastors, Olorisa and Babalawos[5], guidance counselors, best friends, peeps and crews etc. even religions, just the way we change our socks. We need fresh, interesting, impressive answers to keep us on our moral toes. As they say these days 'context is everything,' so even religion has to make sense. But you know something? There is a saving grace here. For many of us, including those young Olorisa on a Brooklyn street corner, our search for an understanding of morality -- of the <u>meaning</u> of Orisa – is not only unending, it is the *beginning* of morality, the beginning of good sense, the beginning of Godliness, the beginning of survival. In this sense I and my esteemed Nigerian co-author Ademola Fabunmi hope that this book will be a source of fascination for our ever searching children, as well as for we their ever searching parents and everyone else involved in or interested in Yoruba Traditional Religion. We also hope that many others will find this collection of "funny stories" enjoyable and somehow useful. So let's get started.

# PREFACE

Let me ask you, did you ever wonder....exactly **who** came up with this right or wrong business? Well, I did too, and after asking Babalawos and Olorisa, from Cuba, the United States and Africa, I still wasn't satisfied that there was a specific code of morals in Yoruba Traditional Religion. But finally one day I asked the same question of Ademola Fabunmi, a highly regarded and very senior Lagos based Babalawo. He simply cocked his head to one side and declared "But every Odu of Ifa contains a lesson in Morality."[6] (I think you know that Ifa is one of the Divine Oracles on which the ancient religion of the Yoruba people is based. And that simply put, an "Odu" is a living chapter in that Oral Scripture.)

I smiled patiently. In reality the beauty and the depth of African religious expression was one of the reasons I converted to Yoruba Tradition in the first place. But at the moment beauty wasn't what I was looking for. "In these times" I explained. "People need a simple and easy reference for things, not riddles and poems -- or else they won't be held responsible for their actions."

"Oh, you mean something like *The Ten Commandments!*" Ademola said, scratching his head. "Well, we have two hundred and fifty-six Odu so there are two hundred and fifty six commandments, isn't that better!?"[7]

"Well, yes and no," I replied, pleased that he knew what I was looking for.

Ademola is the Aseda of Ijo Orunmilla[8] in Lagos which makes him a Babalawo of considerable standing. He is also a very close personal friend who finds my slant

on our mutual religion as fascinating as I find his. Back in the 1930's when Yoruba Traditional Religion was still highly respected among most Lagosians, though Ademola's parents were prominent traditional religious leaders, they sent him to Catholic school to learn to read and write. But still, responding to the condemnation of traditional religion by Christian missionaries bent on colonizing and enslaving the minds of African people while constructing elaborate churches throughout Africa, in 1939 they helped establish the Ijo Orunmilla specifically to teach moral lessons derived from Ifa.

Realizing that I had found what I was looking for I simply said, "My brother, even in Africa traditional priests and even parents no longer speak to their kids in traditional parables and riddles that apply to nearly everything. I mean what do our kids know of even Uncle Remus or Kwaku Ananse?

"Remus?"

"Never mind. And if they do, few remember the source. Young people need all of the information they can get as they grow into a world that we will never know."

"So, what do we do"? Ademola asked, understanding the challenge and sensing that we were about to embark on a new path altogether. I grabbed the moment.

"Well, since sixteen is the sacred number of our religion, why don't <u>you</u> select sixteen Ese Ifa that have to do with morals?" (Ese Fa are the parable like stories within the Odu). I will edit them and get them published in the form of a book that will go everywhere in the world."

"You think your kids in Brooklyn will like it?" He asked.

"Of course they will, they even asked for it!"

"It is done!" Ademola said.

A few weeks later, in his own handwritten Yoruba, my friend and now co-author Ademola Fabunmi delivered what amounts to the original manuscript of this book. However, since his written Yoruba was seriously "old school" I wondered who would be able to translate it into English?

**ACKNOWLEDGEMENTS**

As it happened, my Godson,[9] Joe (Joe T) Quinones, who was studying for a Masters Degree in Religion at the Obafemi Awolowo University in Ile-Ife volunteered to find a translator and to finance the translations as well. He selected another famed Babalawo named Bayo Ogundijo, then a teaching assistant in the renowned Institute of Cultural Studies at OAU. But, even then, it was only after months of further editing Bayo's "English" into English that the first draft of this book was produced. And even then my ever questioning African Canadian Babalawo friend and first reader, Kori Ifaloju Awoyinfa, insisted that my wife Taiwo check over the Yoruba language passages and indeed she must have made a hundred more amendments and corrections. We should mention with respect and sadness that before this book was published Bayo Ogundijo joined his ancestors. Our continued work is dedicated to his memory. And then there was Mama Oseye Mchawi and Mama (Dr.) Shadidi Beatrice Kinsey who housed my body and my soul while I finished it off, Mama Naima Champ who patiently raised funds to print it, Ed Dessisso, the final reader and Brother John Mason who told me about self publishing.

And then there came Aunty Ke-Ke (Karen Quinones-Miller) who, by the way, took me to the river forty-three years ago. Now a veteran columnist with the *Philadelphia Inquirer,* an influential blogger, with a publishing company of her own and a string of best selling novels to her credit, Ke-Ke said "So why don't you publish this thing?"

"OK, let's do it" I said.

"No <u>you</u> do it!" She said. Thanks Ke-Ke for taking me to the river again. You said that giving this book its first real edit was *a labor of Love*. That's what being an Olorisa is…a labor of love.

And let me not forget those 40 year old kids? up there who will read these "funny stories" to their own children. And Kikelomo, Babajide and Ololade (my own brood) let me just say…If not for you. Thanks to every one of you.

Lloyd Weaver, Lagos/New York
February 2004-September 2016

# INTRODUCTION

"Morality" concerns both our *individual feelings* as well as our *collective beliefs* about how we should or should not behave. Or simply, morality is about right and wrong. But some of us will still ask "what is the *source* of these "feelings and beliefs?" or "I know we have our Oral scripture, our Ifa and Merindillogun as well as our African customs and traditions, but to be honest, I'm really not feeling it."

Well let's face it, the challenge of living African (where you don't look an elder in the eye) while also living western (where transparency and accountability are watchwords no matter who you are) brings confusion. Many of us practice our very African religion in an environment in which the prevailing culture relies on specific sources and *lists* (You know, The Bill of Rights, dress codes and mission statements etc.) by which constancy is assured in all aspects of life. But for African Americans and other marginalized communities who find that slavery, oppression and attempted genocide actually thrived under the Ten Commandments, and that the Bill of Rights provides no rights for us, and that most mission statements, corporate or otherwise, are not written with us in mind, too often we have to play it by ear in deciphering our own right from wrong. In fact, that's how some of us found our way *back* to African Religion in the first place. So, if only as an exercise those of us in the socio/political/spiritual war trenches have a practical question: How do we, as followers of an African belief system know for sure what is moral and what is not? How do we get away from the western insistence on lists and move our heads into an African way of seeing life and the world around us?

Not easy. Linguists, philosophers and every day Yorubas have said that in the Yoruba language there is no word for morality! That the closest to it is probably *Iwa*, or *character*. You see? So the problem is not how to speak in another person's tongue, it's how to think in another person's *culture*. How the "another person" can become you. So the question: For those disposed to African traditional spirituality, does that mean we have no rules? The answer: Sometimes we complain that we have too many rules. It's just that our expectations concerning one another's behavior, concerning the question of Iwa, <u>doesn't end with rules</u>.

Seemingly, the most fundamental manifestation of African culture has been in the insistence on *respect*. Respect for elders and parents, respect for the environment we live in, respect for ourselves. But even while that works, somehow there has to be more. Shouldn't the cultural imperatives of morality expressed as *respect* be delineated somewhere? In most societies the definitions of moral behavior are found clearly and conveniently listed in scripture, i.e. our Bibles and Holy Qurans and Torahs, and Bhagavad Gitas etc. and even going back to what might have been the first sacred text, the Maat contained in the Husia of ancient Egypt (Kemet). Since ancient times such sacred sources have been recognized as *The Word of God* because…they *are*. And of course, in case you are wondering, the countless lessons contained in the Odu of Ifa and Owo Merindillogun of Yoruba Traditional Religion provide the basis for the moral instruction given by our learned Orisa priests and philosophers, our teachers, parents, and other elders as well. These oral texts give us consistency and order. In the beauty of their expression, they bind us together.

As said though, for Arican American adherents of an African spiritual culture there are challenges. The need to reconcile the imperatives of African culture requiring unmitigated respect for elders while also heeding the need for "transparency" in a modern world where everyone has a camera phone and a facebook account and the truth is in your face all of the time.

But what does that mean in actual practice? Where and how do our own African derived cultural imperatives define the way that we use these tools? Do we discard the intimate African systems of checks and balances as even our elders come under scrutiny? Do we sacrifice our dignity and cultural propriety just because we are right? Must traditional values yield to a world in which the justice system provides no justice, but the public glare demands it? Or is right and wrong to be confused by claims of propriety? Obviously there is something to be said for an insistence on transparency and accountability and after all doesn't a good question deserve an answer? Our shared assets, including our faith and its customs are sacred or civil trusts. And too, the raising of children is a sacred and communal trust. So let's be clear.

In African society *awo* refers to the inner sanctum of the most sacred trust and to the people allowed into it. It is where Divinity holds court and issues are handled with coolness. "Inside" is not where elders, Babalawos, Olorisa, Oloyes, Obas, Oloris, Aremos etc. *hide* when their behavior is questionable…rather it is a place where ones, <u>anyone's</u>, ass might be kicked for being morally wrong. There is an implied oath among awos. That while what is inside is inside, what is right is right and what is wrong is wrong.

In this way we appear to the world as a moral force because we have promised to be one on the inside. That is a moral code, too. Culture, inscribed by discretion in an African sense, is what the stories in this book are about.

Okay. But still many of us who live outside of Africa will ask "From where in our scripture do those of us who adhere to Yoruba Traditional Religion derive our understanding of what is moral and what is not?" Clearly in Ifa and Merindillogun there are no specific *lists*. Yet, the most casual look at African society reveals a constant emphasis on discipline and on moral principles of behavior. We give deep respect to our elders, we respect one another's property, we care for, feed and instruct one another's children, we do not commit adultery, we dress with flash and style but with modesty, we contribute to one anothers well being, we care for the unfortunate, we share everything. We are, in every way, a moral people. But still, where do we derive our common understanding of right and wrong?

We have said it. The answer is both complex and simple. Without ever using the word "morality" each of the sixteen Odu of Ifa and Merindillogun, and *each* of the two hundred and fifty-six chapters called Omo Odu and the four thousand and ninety six classical verses and the evolved others called Ese Ifa in Ifa or Apataki or Itan in Merindillogun, speak of one or more moral issues. To merely be in the environment of this religion is to gain an overview that we are beholden to reflect in our behavior. However, given the complex environment of the modern world that most of us live in, this book helps *illustrate* the where and the how every Odu describes morality by presenting sixteen selected Ese Ifa from the four thousand and ninety six plus. Certainly, while we will see many differences between the outlook of African religions and other religions of the world, we will also see that these differences are primarily *cultural,* and in reality, there are no differences.

From ancient times African people have understood a moral sense as something that we are born with. With morality, or an understanding of it, taken for granted, greater emphasis is put on the "brother" of morality which Yorubas refer to as *good character*. What is the difference? Most Yorubas will say that *morality* is the principle that you aspire to, *character* is what you do or how you behave. In Yoruba society, it is one's "character" that we constantly hear and speak of. In the Yoruba language the word for "character" is *Iwa,* and "good character" is called *Iwa rere.* (For those who are still wondering, Iwa Rere and Iwa Pele are the same thing).

There is a proverb that all Yoruba children learn, "Iwa Rere l'aso Eniyan." This translates to "Good character is the cloth that covers the Children of The World.[10]" Iwa Rere has to do with how the innate goodness in each of us <u>becomes apparent in our behavior</u> and the way that we carry ourselves. In other words, "good" Iwa can be seen in our outward behavior; it is just there, we wear it as we wear our clothing, but if it is real it is far more difficult to remove.

But to really understand Iwa Rere, you must know that just as we can change our our clothing at will, it is *possible* to change bad or undesirable character for good. To put aside behavior that is immoral and destructive to society. As an example, since we Africans believe that Olodumare gave us the ability to change destiny through prayer (adura) and sacrifice (ebo or adimu), we are told that through ebo[11] we can be forgiven and receive Divine assistance in achieving change. But first we must learn to forgive others. This is where morality comes in. We must deliberately *assume the posture and behavior* of Iwa Rere. In other words, we must strive to clean up our own acts.

For instance, while it is okay to pray for our own individual strength and for success, it is still immoral to pray to Olodumare or to the Orisa for undue advantage over our competitors, or to hope that our competitors will fail or come to harm. This is how an African at his best thinks. And so, even in a society defined by a tradition of white supremacy, when ones every prayer includes a wish to defeat the enemy that denies us a place of honor and equality, that unjustly imprisons us and scatters our communities, that demeans us in media causing us sometimes to even hate ourselves, it is difficult to discern between <u>competitior</u> and <u>enemy</u>, but one of our greatest and most consistent prayers is for *ire isegun ota*, strength to defeat our enemies. But who is an <u>enemy</u> as opposed to someone we don't like? Is it immoral to acknowledge theat white people are the enemy of black people? And perhaps vice versa? Let us know what we are praying for because our prayers will surely work. On the same hand, we should be sure to praise and to thank Olodumare and the Orisa for the blessings of life and for the well being of our families, our neighbors and even of our competitors who are also Children of God.

Perhaps we can now see that even our Iwa depends on our seen and unseen moral conduct. Even our thoughts. Some Priests would even say that Morality and Character, are the same thing. For many of us, it is only we ourselves and our Orisa who know if our Iwa is truly "rere" or not. It is only we, as individuals, who really know if we ourselves are moral.

This book is about morality, or character, as described in Yoruba Traditional Religion. In the chapters which follow, there are only sixteen out of thousands of examples of what one Yoruba scripture, Ifa, says about what is right and what is wrong. They are just the ones Ademola chose. The Odu of Merindillogun[12] offers the same insight and wisdom, often with different, but always equally fascinating, stories (Apataki). Why Ifa instead of Merindillogun? Well, Why not? Enjoy and learn.

# IWA RERE

# CHAPTER ONE

## OGBESE[13]

## **OBATALA AND THE SERVANT**

To honor and respect Olodumare[14] is to honor and respect all of creation…including ourselves. If this is true, and since Olodumare created each of us, certainly we should honor and respect one another. We should strive to know the true talents and the deeper value of others. Even those who are disadvantaged, lacking arms or eyes or good sense, can also have advantages that the rest of us find useful. We know that such people are around us, we see them constantly and if they are needy we must provide for them as we provide for our families and ourselves. We ought not to drive them from our sight. It is *immoral* to do so. We should refrain from judging them because they seem to lack. In time we will see powerful men who, because of their destiny or their mistakes, become paupers; and lame men who because of their goodness or their talents come to buy plots of land and build houses. Indeed, we are told by Olodumare to provide the disabled and disadvantaged with sustenance, and also the *means* of sustenance. It is *moral* to do so and also we never know in what way Olodumare will provide for us through them.

Likewise, those who are disabled must not despise themselves. It is not the wish of Olodumare that they should do so. It is they who know best the ways in which they can be useful to themselves and to society. In these ways a society exists. This is the instruction and the hope of Olodumare whom we all live to please.

Ogbe Ose was the Odu that appeared when Orisanla was about to buy a servant to help him on his farm. It was for Orisanla that the Babalawo chanted this deep Ese Fa called Ogbese.

> "The poverty that grips the Babalawo
> will not end in his death.
> The tatters and scars will one day become riches.
> Surely one day we will remember our hardships
> with laughter."
> Read Ifa for Orisanla Oseregbo before he
> bought Crippleman as his first servant.
>
> Oju to npon Babalawo
> Aponkuko
> Osi to nta Babalawo Atala ni
> Toba pe titi Gbogbo wa loo foro yi serin
> Difa fun Oosanla Oseregbo tio f'Aro sakora Eru
> "Crippleman?"

**NOTE**: *There is a saying in Yorubaland:" If you go to the market to buy yam, buy yam. If you go to the market to buy beans buy beans; but don't stand around staring at the faces of the market women."*

It was in the coolness of the early morning that the busy sellers of Ideti Market poked one another with excitement; their knowing glances said everything. Surely the shuffling entrance of Obatala Oseregbo meant it would be well for them. "Heeepa Baba!" they cried out in delight as The Great Orisa passed.

"E wura O! E pele! Aje O!¹⁵," he responded, acknowledging their respect and good wishes with his own, his smile soft, kind, indulging yet indifferent, his ancient eyes curiously searching above their crowns of fire.

"Kilo fera, Baba? What can we offer you?" each advertised, pompously dusting their wares, white teeth and broad grins betraying their usual shyness…and their curiosity. "What could The Great Orisa be looking for in the market?" A fruit hawker on the still settled path kneels gently. Orisanla passing deftly plucks a tangerine from the tray atop her head, five cowries are left in its place. It is the first sale of the day; the market erupts with joy. The maiden will surely sell her luscious fruit ten times over. "Aje O" (Sell well), Obatala mumbles softly, peeling the fruit as the eleso scurries away. "Eeeee!!" a chorus of merchants cries out with laughter. The Father of our forefathers has opened the market O! Kernels of corn are strewn in his path. Surely they all will prosper.

Step-by-step, into the depths of the market the most venerable Orisa shuffles along remembering and wondering, 'Why had that Orunmilla paused for so long, staring at his opele, then laughing aloud before instructing. "The first servant that you see in the market is the one you should buy o!" What could he have meant? "Ese" (Thank you) Orisanla had answered, rising to leave.

"You should avoid indecision o!" the Babalawo shouted at the old man's back, watching with a pleased smirk as Orisanla bent, groaning as he slowly squeezed his frail shoulders through the small door, then straigtening again to face the dry road to the Oba's market. "Things are seldom what they appear to be." The Babalawo stifled a laugh on hearing Orisanla's creeking bones. And then a final shouted warning "And remember to sacrifice so that things will not go amiss!" Grumbling at the insolence of Orunmilla, Obatala disappeared into the parched road that led to the palace. Branching to the valley called Ideta The Great Orisa did as he was told. He performed the sacrifice of Ogbese.

It was the following morning; with practiced grace, a measure of eku, eja, ori ati agbado, and three atare were dropped on the mound of Esu[16], the Orisa of Chance and Change, as he entered the market. "Kilo fera, Baba!?" the market women called in excited competition as he passed among them. But oddly the old man stopped; the words of the Babalawo echoing in his head. *"The first servant that you see in the market is the one you should buy o!"* he recalled, ignoring the women poking one another again as respectful silence quickly fell on the market. As suddenly as he had stopped, saying nothing, he moved again. The women watched; one by one they gradually smiled in relief and wonder as Orisanla moved through the growing crowd.

It was in the back corner of the market that Orisanla lifted his head. And there, through the morning haze, he saw him. A fine, well built servant squatting on the ground. Orisanla chose the man and paid for him; and here our story begins.

> *"The poverty that grips the Babalawo*
> *will not end in his death.*
>
> *The tatters and scars will one day become riches.*
> *Surely one day we will remember our hardships*
> *with laughter."*
> *Read Ifa for Orisanla Oseregbo before he*
> *bought Crippleman as his first servant.*
>
> *Oju to npon Babalawo*

*Aponkuko*
*Osi to nta Babalawo Atala ni*
*Toba pe titi Gbogbo wa loo foro yi serin*
*Difa fun Oosanla Oseregbo tio f'Aro sakora Eru.*

"Crippleman?"

And that is how it happened. To his surprise, when he told his new servant to follow him Orisanla discovered that the man could not stand up! He had chosen a cripple! Of course the seller of servants had disappeared. Orisanla was uneasy. Why had he not asked the servant to stand before he had paid? After all the Babalawo said.... No, it can't be. Had he not heeded the warning of Orunmilla!? What sort of a thing is this? "O pari![17]" Orisanla thought as Crippleman sat watching him. But in time he remembered Orunmilla's final mysterious words "Things are seldom what they appear to be." The still staring market women rudely clucked their tongues and snapped their fingers above their heads before turning back to their stalls. For them there was money to be made.

Orisanla needed a servant who would work for him on his farm, and Crippleman was the servant he had bought. Having no alternative Orisanla lifted Crippleman onto his back. "Ahhh! O ma se[18] O!" came the cry of the market women as Obatala once again passed their rikety stalls leaving the market.

And thus, this old man, his once famed white clothes now in tatters, carried Crippleman out of the town; through valleys and over hills he shuffled and limped and stumbled, until he arrived home.

"Hmph," he grunted, again recalling the words of the Babalawo as he set Crippleman down in front of his hut. "Things are not always as they seem to be."

Slumping at the foot of a tree he stared at Crippleman and spoke aloud. "Well, we will soon see what will be."

Well what can we say? Come and see wonder. The Great Orisa has a problem O! (But remember it is not nice to laugh at the travails of a God, is it? Cawcawcaw).

So it was Orisanla who was serving Crippleman instead of the other way around. Ha! Orisanla was the one who went to the farm and did the planting. He even did the cooking for Crippleman. Orisanla was the one drawing water. The only thing Crippleman could do was to wash Orisanla's clothes. Until one morning while watching Orisanla pack his farming implements Crippleman called his master, "My lord, please allow me to go to the farm with you so that I can be of help to you." Surprised, Orisanla wondered what sort of help Crippleman could render him. "I will perform work that is done while sitting," Crippleman said, as if reading his master's thoughts. Orisanla was puzzled. 'Perhaps my servant is a comedian' he thought to himself. 'A story teller' yes, amusement for children.'

"But there are no children on the farm!" he suddenly shouted aloud. Crippleman said nothing. A moment of silence said everything. Orisanla was embarrassed at his own outburst. "Okay, let's go" Orisanla finally said, lifting Crippleman onto his back.

With purple land crabs nipping at his cracked heels, the Great Orisa carried Crippleman all of the way to the farm.

Orisanla nearly dropped Crippleman to the ground and slumped in the shade of a palm grove from exhaustion. Crippleman smiled and told Orisanla that he knew how to weave baskets. So, after he had rested,

Orisanla cut down palm-fronds and placed them in front of his hut so that Crippleman could find them.

On that very morning Crippleman began to weave baskets. At first he wove baskets in the dozens. Soon he wove baskets in the hundreds. Orisanla began to carry Crippleman to the farm everyday, and there Crippleman wove baskets everyday. Passing farmers noticed, and began to buy baskets to carry their produce. The farmers' wives stole the baskets from their husbands to decorate their homes. The farmers bought more. Before long Crippleman became known far and wide for his fine and beautiful baskets. While Orisanla had never thought of becoming rich, with his baskets Crippleman soon made it so. Orisanla thought of his Babalawo and smiled. "Things are not always as they seem." And that is how it happened.

*Strange story right? Oh, you think there has to be more. Well, as a matter of fact, there is!*

As it happened, there is a very sacred parrot in Yorubaland called Odidere[19]. Now Odidere is known for its bright red tail feathers known as *koide* which are seen on the crowns of priests and kings. Odidere often perched on the trees on Orisanla's farm. Not only did Crippleman know how to weave baskets, but he also knew how to set ropes to trap birds. Soon Crippleman began to capture parrots. From the parrots he caught, Crippleman removed the tail feathers and began to keep them. Soon, just as Crippleman had busied himself weaving baskets and making cages, he also started to weave crowns adorned with the feathers of Odidere.

One day Orunmilla read Ifa for Olofin.[20] Olofin was was asked to offer two hundred tail feathers of

Odidere as sacrifice so that his ailing son could become well again. Olofin's servants searched all of the markets in the kingdom of Olofin but could not find a single parrot's feather. After a while, Esu noticed the servants of Olofin who were searching for the feathers needed by their master. On hearing their plight Esu told them that he knew where to buy the feathers of Odidere and took them to Orisanla's farm. Orisanla told them that he did not have parrot feathers. But his servant Crippleman, said, "My Lord, we do have parrot feathers."

Orisanla was puzzled. "Where are the feathers?" he asked. Crippleman smiled and went to bring them. Orisanla was surprised when he saw the baskets filled with parrot feathers. Each of the feathers was sold for two hundred cowries, making twenty thousand cowries.

Obatala was rich.

*Great story huh? But hold tight, there is more.*

At the palace of Olofin the sacrifice was made with the feathers and Olofin's son rose from his sickness. Now what do you think of that? Olofin was happy and grateful. He thanked Himself. He thanked Orunmilla. He thanked Esu. Olofin sent for another two hundred parrot feathers and paid one million cowries for them. Orisanla became a wealthy man. He too was grateful and shared his wealth with Orunmilla and his diviners.

But then Olofin wished to know the person who supplied the parrot feathers and sent for Orisanla.

As Orisanla was about to leave for Olofin's palace Crippleman asked him to remove his cap from his head. Orisanla was surprised at the request, but curiosity got the best of him and he did as Crippleman asked. Squatting and bending over, Crippleman placed a crown of feathers on the head of Orisanla. Orisanla filled a calabash with water and looked at the reflection of himself. There he saw that he was truly The Great Orisa. He was happy. Orisanla praised himself and he praised his servant:

**Song**
*The servant I bought was a good servant.*
*The servant I bought made me a wealthy man.*
*The servant I bought was a good servant.*

**Orin**
*Eru ti mora leru ire*
*Eru ti mora leru ire*
*Eru ti mora lola mi*
*Eru ti mora leru ire*
*Owo ti mo mu re oja*
*Owo aro ni*

As Orisanla sang, he danced to Olofin's palace. As he passed the market the sellers left their stalls and joined Orisanla, rejoicing all of the eay to the palace of Olofin. On seeing Orisanla, Olofin began to give him more money. Olofin gave Orisanla a house. Olofin gave Orisanla a horse. Olofin named Orisanla "The King of the Crown" (Iko). This was how Orisanla became a wealthy man. He remembered how the Babalawo with the sweet mouth had called Ifa:

"The poverty that grips the Babalawo
will not end in his death.
The tatters and scars will one day become riches
surely one day we will remember our hardships
with laughter."
Read Ifa for Orisanla Oseregbo before he
bought Crippleman as his first servant.

*Oju to npon Babalawo*
*Aponkuko*
*Osi to nta Babalawo Atala ni*
*Toba pe titi Gbogbo wa loo foro yi serin*
*Difa fun Oosanla Oseregbo tio f'Aro sakora Eru.*

**Orin**
*Eru ti mora leru ire*
*Eru ti mora leru ire*
*Eru ti mora lola mi*
*Eru ti mora leru ire*
*Owo ti mo mu re oja*
*Owo aro ni*

This Ese Ifa makes it clear that we should not look down on the disabled...they are a mystery from Olodumare and are the wards of Orisanla. We should give them the opportunity to be useful; we will be surprised at the rewards. A servant should not look down on himself. He should declare who he really is and show his master his true ability. "There is more than dust in the dustbin."

Oh, but before we go I want you to remember that the Babalawo told Obatala to make ebo, and Obatala did. You got that? He gave a portion to Esu leaving nothing for granted and found the person who would create his fortune. Why? Because he knew that it was the right thing to do. And sure enough, in addition to finding the servant who would make him wealthy by weaving baskets, when Olofin's servants looked for parrots feathers, it was Esu who made sure that they went to Orisanla who didn't even know that his servant had gathered all of the feathers in the world. Orisanla had gone to Orunmilla before he set out on a venture that was important. Orunmilla gave him instruction.

Orisanla, though skeptical and arrogant, and himself wiser than the wise, obeyed. But get this. It was in his character to assist and help the servant who was crippled. It was a burden to a man whose age iss measured in centuries, but he did it without hesitation. Ire was his.

*Okay, just want to be sure you got that.*

Aboru Aboye

*\* Esu is the messenger who stands to help anyone who makes sacrifice; though the goodness or blessing may come later than expected. Sometimes Esu will appear as a person in order to bring the reward of the sacrifice. It was Esu who was to bring the reward for Orisanla's obedience when Orisanla was told by the Babalawo to buy Crippleman as a servant, and to keep him as a friend.*

# CHAPTER TWO

## OWORINSOGBE

### **GOODNESS WALKS SLOWLY**

OWORINSOGBE teaches that we should persevere and think deeply about our lives and its meaning because no one knows when their Grace (Ire)[21] will come except Olodumare. If we, the Eniyan (the children of Obatala blessed with the breath of Olodumare), knew the time of our individual Grace, none of us would work again; though it holds that labor is the medicine for poverty. Okay, let's back up a minute and explain a few things. You see, even though creation happened over a period of hundreds of thousands, maybe millions of years, in the way God (Olodumare) looks at it, it happened very fast.[22] He made the Earth and then sent Obatala to make the bodies of people. He gave them the breath of life and they became, through Obatala, God's children. As a society, the children of Obatala covered the Earth, The society, or family of man, is called Eniyan. Now Ire didn't accompany the making of people. (Maybe that idea occurred to God later, I don't know, but that is what this story is about). Anyhow Ire is one of those hard to interpret words in English so sometimes we call it Goodness, Grace, Good things, or even Blessing. You get the picture right? And there are different kinds of Ire. You know like Health, Wealth, Long Life, Money, Children and on and on. Individually and collectively the good things of life are called Ire. Got it? Can we go on? Good because this is a good story.

Ire (Good Things) does not like laziness because it knows not how to assure good health for He-Who-Does-Nothing. He-Who-Lacks-Good-Health can never have Long Life. That is why Oworinsogbe tells us this:

*Saanyan is dancing,*
*Alaari is helping Saanyan.*
*Tete Awo of Iba Igbo, divined for the people of Otu-Ife.*
*They awoke everyday expecting Ire.*

*Saanyan is dancing.*
*Alaari mimes his every move at Otun Moba.*
*Tete Awo of Iba Igbo*
*Made divination for the people of Otun Moba*
*And also for the people of Otu-Ife*
*Who wake up everyday expecting Ire, Good Things.*

*Saanyan njo*
*Alaari ngbe lese*
*Tete Awo Iba Igbo*
*difa fun won l'Otu Ife*
*Fojojumo ji, won nreti ire*

*Saanyan njo*
*Alaari ngbe lese*
*Tete Awo Iba Igbo*
*Difa fun won l'Ode Otun Moba*
*A bufun Lotu'fe won ji won nreti ire*

Confused? Okay try to imagine this: Way back when, in the earliest days of man, the world was not an easy place. Men and women wandered across the continents in search of convenience, security and settlement. They searched and they searched for the Grace and the Goodness that they had been promised in Heaven. There was dust and little rain. Rivers and oceans often seemed far away. Farming was hard. When men and women (Eniyan) found their way across the world, many suffered their journeys in adversity, without vision or hope. Often they cried out to Olodumare. They asked for whatever relief or advantage or blessing they wanted. In desperation the people of Imoba and Otu-Ife (Two neighboring towns) came together and asked their Priests how they could be blessed with Goodness; Oworinsogbe was the Odu that appeared and the chants of the Priests informed the petitioners that Grace was forthcoming; but if over time Grace did not come, they should continue their offerings and their pleadings since it is Grace who brings Goodness with Him.

And it happened. Because of their persistent plea, Olodumare in the Orun (beyond the sky) opened the calabash of Ire and sent the Goodness of Heaven to live with Eniyan on Earth. And so it is remembered:

*When Ire was coming, he brought Aje (Money) along,*
*Aje brought Wife.*
*Wife took child along,*
*And Child took with him Home.*
*Home brought with him Horse.*

*Igba ti Ire nbo omun Aje lowo*
*Aje mun Aya lowo*
*Aya mun Omo lowo*
*Omo mun Ile lowo*
*Ile mun Esin lowo*

Goodness walks slowly. Alas, it took him three full Dry Seasons before he reached Earth, because he was never in haste while walking.

But they knew. The Priests who divined for the people of Otunmoba and Otu-Ife had told them to be hard working, taking little time to rest, because Goodness hates laziness. On hearing this, the people of the two towns began working without hesitation knowing not when Goodness would come. However, it was not long before the people of Otunmoba became fed up. They said to one another, "The Goodness that we have been expecting for two years has not come." In their homes and in the farmland and in meetings they complained of endless waiting. "Since Goodness has not come, and since we have never rested, no one can say that we are lazy," they said. "One should not be lazy not knowing the time when Goodness will arrive." And so they began to take their rest at night. Can anyone say they became lazy?

Goodness walks slowly. Alas, it took him not two, but three full Dry Seasons before he reached Earth, because he was never in haste while walking.

When Goodness left Heaven, he first arrived at Otunmoba. Goodness arrived at Otunmoba with Aje. Aje brought Wife. Wife took Child; and Child brought with him Home. Home brought with him Horse. When Goodness, Aje, Wife, Child, Home and Horse met the people of Otunmoba, the people of Otunmoba had slept off; everywhere in the city there was silence because when Goodness arrived in Otunmoba all of the people were sleeping. May Olodumare never let our Goodness pass us by. The people of Otunmoba had slept off. Goodness had to wait. He dismantled his wares.

"Certainly, sooner or later, they will wake up." Goodness waited and waited until it was morrow time. And still the people of Otunmoba did not wake up because they were too tired. So Goodness, and all of those with whom he traveled to Earth, left Otunmoba.

In the early evening Goodness arrived at Otu-Ife. As though labor were the same as food, the people of Otu-Ife worked both day and night. If anyone asked "Why?" to a person they simply answered, "Perseverance often has a Good Ending." Everyone faced their own work; it was nearly dawn before anyone noticed the presence of the Stranger who asked to be led to the Oba's palace.

When he arrived he explained to the Oba that he had arrived from the Orun with the Ase[23] of Goodness that Olodumare had given him. He begged the Oba for a place to stay for he had come to live with them. Without hesitation the Oba told Grace that there was space that he could use between the palace and the barn. The servants of the palace settled Grace in the backyard and began to build a hut. And as Grace opened his bags and baggage at the back of the Oba's palace, Wife suddenly appeared; Long Life and Peace also came out. On seeing this, the Oba sent his gong men around the town chanting that the long expected Grace had arrived. Grace then asked the name of the town that he had first come across on the way. The townspeople replied that it must have been Otunmoba. Grace told them that the people there were too lazy. He had met them sleeping. May Olodumare grant that we do not sleep off the Grace He has sent to us.

It was Grace who said a Lazy Person would not know how to take good care of him. Wife said a Lazy Person would not be able to take good care of Her. Child said He-Who-Has-No-Money will never be able to pet him. Longevity said he's far away from He-Who-Lacks-Sound-Health. Grace said that that was the reason they could not stay long in Otunmoba.

Songs of praise and joy flowed from the people of Otu-Ife. They lifted their hands to dance. They lifted irukere (horsetail of joy) as they sang:

**Song:**
*It was the people of Imoba who slept off!*
*It was the people of Imoba who slept off*
*Ire, Good Things passed them by to Otu Ife*
*It was the people of Imoba who slept.*

**Orin:**
*Ara Imoba losun lo o*
*Ara Imoba losun lo*
*Ire koja lo s'Otu-Ife*
*Ara Imoba losun lo*

It was the sound of song and dance from Otu-Ife that awakened them at Otunmoba. "What made the people at Ife dance so joyously?" they wondered. They ran to their Priests and their Priests said "Have we not told you not to be down hearted; that you should continue working both day and night, though no one knows when the Visitor will arrive?"

The people of Otunmoba began to regret their laziness. The people of Otu-Ife were dancing and giving praise to Olodumare. They praised their Priests who had used their divine tongues to chant Ifa:

*Saanyan is dancing.*
*Alaari is helping Saanyan. Tete Awo of Iba Igbo.*
*They also divined for them at Otu-Ife.*
*They awoke everyday expecting Ire, Good Things,*

*It was the people of Imoba who slept off*
*It was the people of Imoba who slept off*
*Ire, Good Things passed them by to Otu-Ife*
*It was the people of Imoba who slept off.*

*Saanyan njo*
*Alaari ngbe lese Tete Awo Iba Igbo*
*Difa fun won l'Otu Ife*
*Fojojumo ji, won nreti ire*

*Ara Imoba losun lo o*
*Ara Imoba losun lo*
*Ire koja lo s'Otu Ife*
*Ara Imoba losun lo*

This parable of Ifa teaches us to work persistently, sometimes without resting, and to have Perseverance and Faith. No one knows when the Visitor will come; and so we should continue to labor and never be lazy or doubtful of our destiny. And also, just because you made ebo and worked hard, don't be downhearted when your Ire doesn't just jump up in your face. Olodumasre's clock is sometimes a bit different than ours or maybe, sometimes, he just goes to sleep. Just kidding!

Aboru Aboye.

# Chapter Three

## OTURA OBARA (OTUA RABA)

### THE WAY OF BROTHERS

Who teaches the birds to move as one?

Who tells the fish to school together?
Surely antelopes are not told to heed the signal.

It is only we, The Children of the World (Eniyan) who are <u>told</u> that without cooperation and collaboration we will not see the

Grace of our Father Olodumare.

Otua Raba reminds us that like the birds and the fish and the antelope, we too must work together for accomplishment and for our common salvation. Love brings fidelity between brothers and sisters. Between neighbors, reliability and devotion brings about trust and trustworthiness. These are the ingredients of success. Our foreparents said, "A well-tied broom disrupts the gourd of flies." If we as *friends* work together for our progress, surely we as *individuals* will benefit.

Our strength is in our unity, Otua Raba puts it this way.....

*The hands of the young do not reach the high shelf*
*The hands of the Elders cannot enter the small gourd*
*Let the Elder not reject their children*
*Likewise let the child also know his duty*
*Made divination for Otua and Obara*
*When they were making a trip to Kisi…*

*Owo Ewe won oto pepe*
*Tagba lagba kowo akeregbe*
*Ise ewe bagba, komai ko mo*
*A ma lohun ti baba se fomo*
*Di fa f'otua oun obara*
*Won sa wo re ile kisi…*

Both Otua and Obara visited their Priests seeking advice about their journey. How might they find prosperity? What might be their undoing? The Priests told them that, "If only you remember to cooperate and have respect for one and other, surely you will bring back ample gain. Remember that one good turn deserves another and two hands will always wash clean. If you fail to cooperate, to help one another and to work together, you both will surely regret it."

When they arrived at Kisi, Otua soon took to the work of midwifery. Obara busied himself making prayer and sacrifice for people. Though they both did well, they did not see what they had in common and went their separate ways, refusing to work hand in hand.

"Can't you see I'm too busy to help you." Otua said to Obara, "And why are you here? What do you know of medicine?"

"You only want to steal my clients," Obara accused his brother, "My fame will reach home and I will have honor."

Neither wanted the other to become more prosperous than himself. If an expectant mother came to Obara seeking the safe delivery of her child, Obara would surely send her to someone other than Otua. In this way he could be sure that Otua would not become richer than he. On the same hand, if someone came to Otua seeking counsel in order to improve his life, rather than sending the supplicant to his brother Obara, Otua would vigorously advertise the benefits of another diviner. In this way, Otua would insure that Obara would never become richer than he.

Both Otua and Obara continued to deny each others assistance. Rather, each would do all imagineable to assure that the other would never see prosperity. In this way neither achieved progress. For three years, no progress for Otua. For three years, no progress for Obara. One day, haggard and starving, both Otua and Obara were forced to leave Kisi and return home. When they arrived, each went to their Priests. The patient and forgiving Babalawos read Ifa for them again:

The Goodness of one is in the hand of the other. Ifa said that Otua and Obara should have Love for one another and that unless they cooperate and work together, neither would prosper as an individual. Both Otua and Obara returned to Kisi together. But this time each resolved to always advertise the Goodness of the other. And this they did. If a supplicant came to Otua seeking to make sacrifice for his Well Being, Otua would send him to Obara for divination and sacrifice. When things turned out well the supplicant would always return to Obara to show his appreciation with money and gifts. Obara would then share his Reward with Otua.

Also, if a patient came to Obara for child delivery, Obara would clearly state that this is not his work. Rather he would boast of his brother, Otua, who was the best midwife in the land. Of course, Otua would always do a splendid job. In this way the Reputations of Otua and Obara both grew and clients and patients came from far and wide seeking their services. Both of them became great. Later, both Otua and Obara came to live together in one place. Before long they combined their work together. After a time they became famous and all of the people of Kisi praised them for their work and for the example they set by cooperating and working together. Before a year had passed they had become well-to-do. If one of them went to his hometown the other would stay to make money for the other. Each was able to build a house and to purchase land for farming outside of the town. Each aquired horses of different colors.

When Obara and Otua returned to their hometown, the way of their wealth was a lesson to all to work in unity and to find ways of improving the lot of the other. And that they should struggle to find Goodness for one another and avoid envy. That if one looks for the Goodness of the other, surely he shall receive his own Goodness in return.

In this way Otua and Obara came to realize that, "One good turn deserves another" and that "Each hand washes the other clean." They began to praise their Priests; their Priests were praising Ifa. And this is what they said:

*The hands of the young do not reach the high shelf.
The hands of the Elders cannot enter small gourd.
Let the Elder not reject their children.
Likewise let the child also know his duty.*

*Made divination for Otua and Obara when they were making a trip to Kisi.
Let Otua and Obara know
that Ifa Priests are never put to shame in any land."*

*Owo Ewe won oto pepe
Tagba lagba kowo akeregbe
Ise ewe bagba, komai ko mo
A ma lohun ti baba se fomo
Di fa f'otua oun obara
Won sa wo re ile kisi
Otua o obara Awo kiite, nile kile.*

**Song:**
*Otua Obara
Otua Obara
Awo does not experience shame anywhere*

**Orin:**
*Otua oo Obara
Otua ooo Obara aa
Awo Kiite nile kile o*

Cute story right? But rather obvious. But whatever you do please, please don't you ever forget it. The bit about children needing help to reach the high shelf, and elders not being able to get their hands into the small gourd is actually a common and enduring saying in Nigeria and its popularity is one of the reasons it is included in our sixteen stories. Now when you see people messing up by not cooperating you might use the quip "Backwards ever, forward never." Familiar? Look at it again. I like that one too because it's funny. But the point is, if we don't work together we ain't going nowhere. No where. And the ability to help others and work together toward common goals is a good sign of your Iwa Rere. So as my father used to say "Now put <u>that</u> in your pipe and smoke it." Or as we say...

Aboru Aboye

# Chapter Four

## IRETE OTUA

### **IWA RERE**

This Odu Ifa warns mothers to exhibit great character in raising their children. But take it easy o!

*Take it easy? So what does that mean?*

To be a mother is no simple thing, it is a task never mastered. Remember in the introduction to this book we wondered about the "source of morality." We said that for Yorubas, morality and good character were the same, and could be seen as easily as the clothes that we wear.

But the question remains, how do we know the *rules of life*? Who teaches us how to dress? And where do we get the discipline and the flow that defines us as good people? Now don't say "instinct." Clearly, *behavior* is the cloth of character and behavior is *learned* from one's....now say it, Mother! Good!

So sorry ladies, it's all your fault or your glory. So, before you put this book away let's talk about it. Why? Because the reward of your success is the eternal love and gratitude of your child. And just as important, the reward of your success is your child's contribution to the progress and cohesion of the community. If your child has good character, yes, take pride in yourself because <u>you</u> passed it on.

"But how can we be sure?" you ask. "Weren't we told that we choose our destiny in the Orun before coming to theis world?" Nobody gives it to us. But when we need a quick fix, we Africans believe that mothers have the *magic*; it is they who can even change the destiny of their children. Now, without getting you're your (mother's) secrets Irete Otua tells us further that indeed, the ways of mothers are many. They say that mothering itself is an instinct (that word again) and not a thing to be learned. But Irete Otua warns our mothers...while you should always pamper your children, you should take even greater care not to spoil them with leniency that does not reflect life's realities. It is the work of the mother that will determine whether or not the child will be useful to himself and to his town. Eh heh! We know. Life's joy is also life's burden!

An untrained child will sell the house that was built by his father; he will also sell the vehicle owned by his brother. Such a child, we are told, will surely be unprogressive. Oh pari!

But in the end Irete Otua tells us that the character of the child reflects the character of the mother; that we should not train our children with a double tongue. It is no simple thing though, and we must never be sullen or complacent or discouraged. Rather we should be forever insistent, and vigilant, and conscious that years go by quickly. Irete Otua begs you....we should not allow our own Goodness, or "Blessing" to pass the world by. Oh, the Blessing here is the Blessing of *children*.

What is worth teaching should be taught constantly, because the child is the expression of the mother. Irete Otua says:

*Goodness in front,*
*Joy at the back.*

*Made divination for Ologoose the relation of Okin.*
*These were the two birds of whom Ifa now speaks.*

*Ire niwaju*
*Ayo leyin*
*Difa fun Ologose oluku Okin*
*Awon ni Eiye meji ti 'fa soro le lori*

Ologose (swan) and Okin (peacock) were both princes, sons of the same king. Ologose was the Elder of the king's many children while Okin was the next in line. *Omoba, (child of the king)* is the title and the joy of princesses and princes alike; the palace court is always alive with the songs and the laughter of the king's many children and the shrill voices of the many mothers whose shouts and warnings are lost in the laughter that echoes through the corridors and the kitchens and everywhere. While the mothers of the compound raise all of their children together, the mother of Okin paid particular attention to her own first born son, training him in what she felt was the "proper" behavior of royalty. She taught him to be neat; to display the traditional forms of politeness to relatives and to those who were not of the royal lineage alike, both at home and on the farm. She taught Okin that to achieve anything in life one should perform one's work and carry out one's business faithfully and with integrity.

Iya Okin trained her son as if he were not a prince at all. When servants at the palace took up their baskets in the morning, Okin's mother would awaken her child also, insisting that he follow them to the farm. Whenever Okin erred and was properly blamed for his wrongdoing, either by his father or by any other person, Okin's mother would also blame her child for the wrongdoing, never siding with him when he was wrong. Sometimes Okin wondered if he was truly born to the woman he was told was his mother. Okin longed to be pampered as other children were.

On the other hand, Okin's elder brother, Ologose, always enjoyed the best of life. In addition to "Omoba," Ologose had another, very special title. He was known as *Aremo*, the eldest son of the king. And this was his mother's pride. Ologose woke up late everyday; he did no work. His mother merely placed his food by his sleeping mat and he ate without even taking a bath. Whenever he was called upon to go to the farm, Ologose's mother would refuse to allow him to go declaring that he was a prince, and Aremo at that, and not a servant. Hardly did Ologose cut his hair or trim his fingernails. And whenever he offended and was flogged by his father his mother would cry out to people to warn the king not to kill her child. If an outsider blamed this child for wrong doing that person would certainly be railed and punished by Ologose's mother who, after all, was *Oloriagba*, a queen among queens.

In this way Ologose became a spoiled child. He never did anything on time. He was always dirty, ill-mannered, and all who knew him secretly looked down on him. That is, except his mother. And in this way life in the palace continued.... until that fateful day, Baba Ologose joined his ancestors or, as we sometimes say, "The Oba entered the roof." The burial ceremonies were long and mysterious. But the public funeral was a splendid celebration of a life that had been well spent. For several months the people alternately mourned and celebrated. But one day all of the ceremonies ended and it was time for the townspeople to choose another Oba.

But really, there was no "choosing" to be done. You see, the selection of kings in this part of Yorubaland followed the customs of Benin from where many families traced their origins. Rather than the Obaship rotating among the families of the founders of the kingdom, it was a father to son affair. No hassle, no tussle. The late Oba's eldest son was his unquestioned successor.

To all of the townspeople it was clear that Aremo Ologose would soon become their king. The eldest of the Babalawos of the town knew that there was only one candidate for the throne. Ifa was only consulted to determine the date. But when they asked there it was…Irete Otua. The Kingmakers, shook their heads with expressions of concern….but said nothing; it was theirs to agree on the procedure including the offerings to the calabash of character. "The reign of the next king would be auspicious and successful," they told the townspeople. And that was all that they said. And soon the day that they would crown their Oba was announced.

When that was done, following tradition, the kingmakers came to tell Ologoshe of the ceremonies he would undergo. He was told that it was the local practice to keep the power, or *Ase* of the town, somewhere outside the town gate, and that the Oba-to-be would have to go and search for it and bring it back before he would take his title bath. He was also told that early on the day he would search for his Ase the Kingmakers would wait for him to give him a special soap with which he would bathe at the river. This was to be done before dawn; well before the early morning cock crows. They told Ologose that he should rise early in order to meet these expectations.

Now, as we know, to wake up very early was a heavy burden to Ologose. Since he was used to sleeping until midday Ologose took the problem to his mother, who quickly said that since your brother Okin normally wakes up early in order to go to the farm, it is he who will collect the power of the town and carry the soap to the river for you. *Do you see where we are going?*

Early on the given morning the Kingmakers waited quietly by the riverside expecting Ologose to soon arrive, search for and find the Ase and receive the soap. To their surprise, though, it was Okin rather that Ologose who appeared. Quietly they watched as Okin retrieved the Ase and then asked the kingmakers for the soap that would he had been instructed to keep for his brother. The kingmakers did so, removing the soap from the leaves and placing it in Okin's still wet hand. But then as the kingmakers started to leave, Okin began to wash away the soap that had begin to stain his hands. Noticing that the soap did not go away, Okin began to wipe his hands on his legs. As he did so, his legs became dazzling white. He then attempted to remove the soap from his hands by wiping them on his head, following which the peculiar hair of chieftaincy began to grow. The Kingmakers, heafring Okin's shouts of distress, turned back and shouted "Kabiyesi O!" or "Long Live The King!"

Okin became frightened and embarrassed. He explained to the Elders of the Town that his elder brother Ologose was on his way. And that it was for him that he retrieved the soap. The Kingmakers replied that since he was the one who brought the soap from the secret place, and since the hair of chieftaincy had already grown on his head, that his elder brother Ologose had lost his chance to become Oba. They explained that according to their ancient custom anyone with whom they met the power (Ase) of the town would be the one to be crowned Oba. "There can never be two kings on the throne at the same time," they said. "Therefore, you are our next king."

The ceremonies of chieftaincy began immediately for Okin. But as the sun rose high in the sky they were soon interrupted as Ologose emerged from the town and entered the sacred grove of the Kingd maskers with drummers and praise singers and hundreds of dancing townspeople. On seeing the throng of citizens the kingmakers stopped the highly secret ceremonies to tell Ologose and his followers that the chieftaincy title was a serious matter and that since it was Okin who found and carried the Ase and bathed with the soap it was he who that they recognized as Oba elect.

With great sadness Ologose left the sacred grove of chieftaincy and his younger brother Okin was crowned Oba. It was Okin who entered the secret rooms of the palace where the powers of the Oba were conferred on him. At the appropriate time he was brought before his people wearing his crown and all of the people shouted and hailed their worthy and beloved Oba.

It was then that Okin realized the value of what his mother had taught him. It was then that he began to sing:

**Song**
*Mother makes the wealth of the child*
*Mother makes the wealth of the child*
*My mother made sacrifice and I became wealthy,*
*Mother makes the wealth of child*

**Orin:**
*Iye omo loloro omo*
*Iye omo loloro omo*
*Iya mi ru o emi doloro*
*Iye omo loloro omo*

All the townspeople sang this song with Okin. Ologose was also there and tears ran freely down his face. He finally realized that the reason for his downfall was the permissive way in which his mother had raised him. Had mother taught him to be dutiful and hard working as she had with Okin he would have achieved the throne himself rather than leaving the honor left by his father for his younger brother. Ologose then said that he had a song to sing and that people should sing with him:

**Song:**
*Mother determines the poverty of her child*
*Mother determines the poverty of her child*
*My own mother did not make sacrifice and I became poor.*
*Mother determines the poverty of her child."*

**Orin:**
*Iye omo lolosi omo*
*Iye omo lolosi omo*
*Iya mi oruo omo dolosi*
*Iye mi lolosi omo*

All of the townpeople kept silent, they could not sing with him. Rather, they all turned their heads to look at Ologose's mother. On that day she, Oloriagba, was put to shame. This sacred Ifa corpus teaches us that it is "The mother of the child who makes the wealth of child." Also "It is the mother of child who determines the poverty of child." And so, as a matter of morality –or Iwa – teach

your child well so he can give you rest and you will eat the fruit of your labor in your latter days.
    Ssshhhh! Mother makes the wealth of her child.


Aboru Aboye.

# Chapter Five

## IROSUN OFUN (IROSUN AFIN)

### OLUROUNBI'S PROMISE

Don't you know that life itself belongs to Olodumare? It is not yours to give or to use for barter or to take to the pawn shop. It is the Orisa who will always protect life. Because life itself *is* Olodumare, we have no right to reject it or to give it to others unless Olodumare says so. And He will never say so. This is the pact that we bring to this world. Irosun Afin is the Odu of Ifa that tells us not to promise what is not ours to promise. Irosun Afin is the Odu that tells us not to promise what we will regret giving. It tells us that life itself is Ire (A grace from Olodumare), and that even in those moments of great want we are *responsible* for our utterances.

Irosun Afin tells us that as a matter of "morality" we should carefully consider bargaining ourselves into debt that during times of weakness. We should not make promises that will bring suffering beyond the problem we seek to solve. Neither should we make promises that we will never be able to keep. It is a burden to have made a vow that cannot be kept. One will never have rest of mind in the face of monumental debt. Let us desist from vain or desperate promises. Such an oath will never bring good.

This is how Irosun Afin warns us to avoid vain promises:

*Igbongbon Ada cannot meet with Akika Tree.*
*Divined for Olurounbi child of Saloro of Ijesa.*
*She who shall give herself away*
*to Iroko-Ogbo of Oluwere Forest*

*Igbongbon Ada ose mun Kon Igi Akika loju*
*Adifa fun Olurounbi Omo Saloro ni Ijesa*
*Eyi to yo fenu ara re Fi ara re toro*
*Fun Iroko ogbo, oko Oluwere*

The years of our lives pass into wishes fulfilled and wishes best forgotten. That is life. However Olurounbi, the daughter of a famous chief known as Saloro, was fast growing into old age. Despite her advancing years and long marriage, Olurounbi had never born a child. It was this that troubled her very much. The Ifa Priests warned her to beware the cruelty of Eniyan. That she should not be driven to desperation by the taunts of others. That she should trust the Giver of Life and be happy with His most precious gift. <u>Her own life</u>. But Olurounbi did not listen. Her own unfulfilled wish could not be forgotten and she suffered beyond measure. Add to that the ridicule and scorn of all around her and you will understand Olorunbi's desperation. Olorunbi was childless. Her husband's family even demanded that she leave his house. Her friends shunned her. Olurounbi was in dire need of a child to reclaim her honor. She worried that she would never have a child of her own and that she would always be miserable. Each of her mates had given birth to children. Each of the children brought gifts to their parents. Some of the children had even had children of their own. But poor Olurounbi had never given birth to even a single child.

One day Olurounbi went to ask Ifa if she would ever give birth to her own child. Olurounbi had thought

of doing this many times, but feared that she would not be able to bear a negative answer. So, in desperation she finally asked if it was still possible for her to give birth or if it was her fate to be childless. Ifa said that in order to end her childlessness that she should pray to the Orisa and make sacrifice. Ifa also warned Olurounbi that she should never make a promise or a vow that she could not keep.

Olurounbi listened and one day she made the sacrifice just as Ifa had advised. But after a year she still had not become pregnant. She became anxious again and began to look elsewhere for a solution. One day Olurounbi heard that on the farm of Oluwere there was an Iroko[24] tree that was known to give children to childless women who prayed and made sacrifices there. Eheh!

And so one day Olurounbi went to the farm of Oluwere and found the famous lroko tree. There she pleaded and pleaded to Iroko that she be given a child. Olurounbi explained that she had divined and given sacrifice times without number. She claimed that Olodumare Himself had treated her unfairly and promised the Iroko[25] tree that if it would give her a child, she would surrender her very life to it in return. She vowed to keep her promise even if the child were to be a born-to-die. Day after day she came to the Iroko tree and repeated her offer. One day, as she made her promises to the Iroko tree, a huge crowd gathered behind her. Many who knew her warned her of the grave consequences of desperate promises. "Be quiet!" Olrounbi shouted in anger. "Is it not you who insults me because of my childlessness? Is it not you who makes me ashamed?"

And then, tearfully, Olurounbi said "Even if the child were to die on the day of its birth, at least people would know that I gave birth to a child."

Every one knew it. Olurounbi's state of childlessness had led to a state of madness. Olurounbi knew well that others had made vows of goats, or of sheep and even lesser things, and had delivered healthy children. She knew that others who never did have children, even after making sacrifice, had found happiness despite the cruelty of Eniyan. But Olurounbi remained desperate. So desperate that one day she even volunteered her very life as the sacrifice for having a child.

And sure enough it happened. Soon Olurounbi found herself pregnant and by the tenth month she gave birth to a healthy son. Olurounbi was very happy. She danced with the child into the street, hiring drummers to show the joy she felt because she finally had a child of her very own. Olurounbi was so happy that she forgot everything else. Even the vow she had made to the Iroko tree. But the Iroko tree did not forget. The Iroko tree expected Olurounbi to fulfill her vow. The Iroko tree waited and waited. But to no avail. Olurounbi did not go back to the Iroko tree to fulfill her promise. So Iroko began to appear in the backyard of Olurounbi's house in the dead of night, night after night. It was then that Olurounbi remembered her promise. In fear she listened inside of her house as Iroko sang:

> Everyone was making vow of goat
> Fat, nice-looking goat
> Everyone was making vow of sheep,
> Robust sheep
> Olurounbi made vow of herself Oh!

*Olurounbi O,*
*Janinjanin Iroko! janinjanin.*


*Olukaluku jeje Ewure,*
*Ewure bele nje*
*Olukuluku jeje Aguntan,*
*Aguntan bolojo*
*Olurounbi jeje arara re Arara re Apon bi epo*
*Olurounbi O,*
*janinjanin, Iroko jainjain\**

    Soon Olurounbi realized that she had to surrender herself to the Iroko tree. "Who will now care for my child?" she wondered. In despair Olurounbi quickly ran out of her house and the Iroko tree began to run after her. She ran and ran, with Iroko close behind her, until finally she came to the house of an Ifa Priest; a place where the Iroko, an Orisa himself, dare not enter uninvited. The Priest reminded Olurounbi that Ifa had warned her not to make vain promises. Vain promises, though they are unwise, still make for a debt. But the Priest prayed for Olurounbi anyhow and made a sacrifice for her. This time Olurounbi made a sacrifice of a goat with the head of Awomo (A crudely carved representation of a persons own head that can absorb negativity) on it. Prayerfully they killed the goat and dropped every bit of its blood on the Sigidi Awomo. Meanwhile, the Iroko tree waited impatiently outside, determined that the shrewd Ifa Priest would not keep him from his due. He waited and he waited until finally Olurounbi came out. Quickly the Iroko tree pounced on her and carried her away to the farm. It was only when he got to the farm that Iroko looked well at what he had taken. He was surprised when he found that he had taken the head of Awomo. Iroko cried aloud. He would have his vengeance he vowed.

Dashing the head of Sigidi Awomo to the ground the Iroko tree set out again for the house of Olurounbi.

But before he got very far he met Esu, the messenger of Olodumare, sitting in the middle of the road. It is Esu who carries all sacrifices and petitions to Olodumare. Esu favored Olurounbi because of the many sacrifices she had offered. Hence Esu rose and warned Iroko not to make jest of himself because, after all, he had already carried the sacrifice home. "No one picks a head twice," Esu reminded Iroko.

Esu explained to Iroko that if he did that, people would begin to run away from him saying that now it is human beings that Orisa kills for sacrifice. Iroko well understood the reasoning of Esu. After all, he was an Orisa, too. lroko accepted the head of the goat instead of the head of Olurounbi. And Olurounbi kept her child. But the shock stayed in the mind of Olurounbi, never giving her any peace until, one day, she died.

The lesson taught by this story is simple. We should never make promises that we will not be able to fulfill. We should not make such promises to human beings as well as to Olodumare and the Orisa. Olorunbi was responsible for her own tragedy. As Ifa says:

*Igbongbon Ada cannot meet with Akika Tree*
*Was the Ifa Priest who read Ifa for Olurounbi, child of Saloro of ljesa.*
*She who shall give herself away*
*to lroko-Ogbo, of Oluwere Forest.*
*Every one was making vows of goat*

*Fat, nice-looking goat.*
*Every one was making vows of sheep,*
*Robust sheep*
*Olurounbi made a vow of herself. Oh!*
*Olurounbi, janinjanin*
*Iroko ! janinjanin.*


*Igbongbon Ada ose mun Kon Igi Akika loju*
*Adifa fun Olurounbi Omo Saloro ni Ijesa*
*Eyi to yo fenu ara re fi ara re toro*
*Fun Iroko ogbo, oko Oluwere*
*Olukaluku jeje Ewure*
*Ewure bele nje*
*Olukuluku jeje Aguntan*
*Aguntan bolojo*
*Olurounbi jeje arara re Arara re Apon bi epo*
*Olurounbi O, janinjanin*
*Iroko jainjain*


Aboru Aboye


*\*Jainjain* is a verbal way of mimicking the peculiar way that Iroko walks.

# CHAPTER SIX

## IRETE OSA

## **THE FROG WHO DANCED TOO SOON**

You know that in Africa we take lessons about life from every living creature. The hippopotamus, the antelope and even the hyena all reflect in their behavior something of the divine order of things. Even in our homes where the mice and the cockroaches challenge us over whose in charge (yuck), we somehow find something that is admirable about them. Something in their habits or in their character or in the ways that they move that we take as instructive. Now notice that I said "nearly." I mean, like take the matter of this other guy... you know, frog. Now we know better than to laugh at anything that Olodumare put on this Earth right? But when it comes to frog that's kind of rough. The sound of night crickets some of us call the music of the night. But the croaking of a frog is just disgusting. Damn. And then, look at how he runs. Hahaha. Now imagine a frog even trying to dance with his no head self. Well okay now let's be cool for a minute. We are not here to laugh at anybody or anything, right? But still, let's see if you can hold onto that when you hear this story. This is how Ademola puts it:

*This Odu Ifa tells us to hold fast to our dignity. Certainly the world is unsafe for those who lack self control. For this reason our leaders must always be level headed. Even when they are most happy, they must be aware of themselves* and all about them. When they are angry, they must be judicious and thoughtful. People depend on their leaders for good example and for their safety.

Irete Osa reminds us. We all love frog because he makes us laugh. But when we notice that even though he has a face he has no head, who among us will follow him? And did you notice? When he sees what he wants to eat, or a beautiful frogette, see how he runs! Even when expressing great joy, we must maintain control so that we do not blunder or lead others to ruin. That is the role of our Ori. We must not spoil our happiness with our joy. Irete Osa also teaches that we should take seriously the teachings of Ifa and not laugh at what Olodumare has created (unless perhaps that is why he created it). May we never misbehave.

This is how Ifa tells us this:

> *When the hair is unkempt,*
> *We call on Owner-of-Razor.*
> *It is when the river overflows its bank*
> *that we call on Paddler.*
> *If Paddler, paddles me no more,*
> *I'll paddle myself.*
> *Read Ifa for Akere-o-keyo (a frog)*
> *Who said he would become the Onisinko.*
> *Tomorrow Akere will become Onisinko. Tomorrow.*
> *But because of over joy, Akere broke his thigh.*

> *Ori lokun*
> *Lanpe alabe*
> *Odo lokun*
> *Lanpe ontugbe*
> *Bontugbe otumi, ngosi turami*

*Difa fakere okeyo*

*To loun o je onisinko Lola*
*Lola Lakere o je onisinko lola*
*Ayo ayoju, Lakere se fi itanda*

Irete Osa tells us that our behaviour should always befit the occasion and be worthy of our position. That despite our joy, one foot should always be on the ground so that those who are not content cannot steal our blessing. Besides, how do we celebrate a *blessing-to-come*? Sometimes it is better that we hold our expectation within us. This is Irete Osa:

Akere-o-keyo (a frog) was a prince at Isinko. One day he visited his Priests to ask Ifa "Will I be crowned Onisinko?" (The King of Isinko) The Ifa Priests told him that he should make sacrifice so that his joy will not spoil his expectation. "You should keep your intentions within you," they added. "And you should also feed Esu." Akere-o-keyo did not heed the warning. One day the Oba of Isinko (Onisinko) joined his ancestors. As the townspeople mourned, Akere-o-keyo joyfully remembered that he was the heir to the throne. Forgetting the warning of Ifa, he jumped and shouted happily in expectation of becoming king! All around him were startled by his sudden expression of happiness. The Ifa Priests quickly ran to him. On seeing the wise men, Akere-o-keyo remembered what Ifa said and held himself quietly. But still, he forgot to feed Esu as we all do when we expect the great things that we have prayed for.

For six days the kingmakers prepared for the coronation ceremonies. The townspeople finished their mourning and prepared for the festivities as well.

Meanwhile, Akere-o-keyo steadfastly repeated to himself the warning of Ifa. However, on the sixth day, the day before he would be fully enthroned as Onisinko, Akere-o-keyo could contain himself no longer. "Besides," he thought, "who can spoil my plans on the day before my crowning?" With a grin he called the gangan drummers from their rehearsal. "Beat the drum for me now!" he commanded. "Listen to me! This is what your drums should say...."

*"Tomorrow, tomorrow, this on-coming day, Akere will become the Onisinko tomorrow."*

And so, right inside of Akere-o-keyo's room, the drumming started. Throughout the town, all activities stopped as everyone strained their ears to listen. Though Akere-o-keyo never noticed, Esu squatted in a corner of the room watching and listening to everything that happened. Soon, as Akere started to dance and to jump, Esu could stand it no longer. Softly, he slipped outside where he turned himself into a man before re-entering the room. The man just stood and watched as Akere danced. Suddenly Akere noticed the stranger who simply said, "Oba-of-Tomorrow, this joy should not be done inside the house all by yourself. Nobody will know what is happening inside. Why not go outside!" The gangan drummers continued drumming as Akere danced into the street.

*"Tomorrow, tomorrow, this on-coming day,*
*Akere will become the Onisinko tomorrow."*

Soon the same man called on him again."Oba-of-Tomorrow," the man said, "as a man of dignity, why not change your clothing so that we can dance around the compound? This way everyone will know what will occur here tomorrow."

Akere-o-keyo followed the man's advice. He dashed back into the house and changed into a grand and colorful agbada. He then continued his dance around the compound.

> *"Tomorrow, tomorrow, this on-coming day, Akere will become the Onisinko tomorrow."*

When Akere-o-keyo returned to the front of the house the man advised him again. "It would be very good if you now danced around the entire town so that all of your subjects will know of your crowning tomorrow."

"A very befitting idea," Akere-o-keyo thought. "And besides, with only a few hours until tomorrow, no one will be able to stop my ceremony."

And so Akere stretched his legs in front. Then Akere stretched his legs in back. Akere leaped high into the air. In fact, Akere danced all over the town while all of the people followed him watching and laughing in wonder. Akere-o-keyo danced and danced as the gangan drummers played and sang:

**Song**
*"Tomorrow, tomorrow,
this on-coming day,
Akere will become the Onisinko tomorrow."*

**Orin**
*Lola,
Lakere yo J'onisinko
Lola*

You should have seen this guy. Akere-o-keyo danced and Akere-o-keyo sang, jumping from one side of the town to the other. He was very happy. And whenever he spotted his strange visitor they danced together. In great joy they danced around the town. After a time they were dancing back home. Just as they drew near to his house Akere-o-keyo danced to the front of the drummers while leaping high into the air, hugher than he had ever leaped before. But, as everyone hailed his great feat, Akere suddenly came crashing down, hitting his foot on a stone. Somehow Akere fell to the ground. Ahh! The drummers stopped playing. The people stopped singing. Akere couldn't get up. The people began to whisper to one another that it was unbefitting joy that caused Akere-o-keyo to fall and even to break his leg. What? On the eve of his coronation Akere-o-keyo had broken his leg!? Ewooo!

As everyone knows, it is customary that no town should enthrone a disabled person as Oba. As soon as the kingmakers heard what had happened they were forced to announce that Akere-o-keyo could no longer be crowned Onisinko. Indeed, they selected another person as Oba. They never mentioned Akere Onisinko again. He has since been called "The Son of Onisinko."

Akere missed the title of Onisinko because, in his joy, he lost his dignity. In his joy he even became disabled. He then began to blame the Ifa Priests. But we all remember what Ifa said:

> *When the head is unkempt,*
> *we call Razorman.*
> *It is when river overflows its bank,*
> *we call on Paddler.*
> *If Paddler paddles me no more*

*I'll paddle myself.*
*Made divination for Akere-o-keyo*
*who said he would be enthroned Onisinko*

*but he failed to behave with dignity.*
*He failed to offer sacrifice.*
*He lost his dignity and broke his leg.*

Don't you see that the words of Ifa have come true?" Poverty never kills. But, Irete Osa cautions, "Don't be over joyous."

*Ori lokun*
*lan palabe*
*Odo lokun*
*lampo Ontugbe*
*Bontugbe otumi n'go si tura mi*
*Difa fun Akere Okeyo*
*To loun oj 'Onisinko Lola*

*Ogbo ruru ebo koru,*
*Ogberu atu kesu kotu*
*Ayo ayo L akere se fi tan da*
*Irete Osa ki lo pe ki amayo layoju*

Hey you, stop laughing. Iwa rere, l'aso eniyan.


Aboru Aboye

# Chapter Seven

## OYEKU KANRAN

### THE DEATH OF ELEKAN

Fighting and bickering are always foolish and show a lack of wisdom. In the story preceding this one, the downfall of frog was his lack of dignity (in case you didn't get the point). He was a clown who provided everyone with amusement, but who nobody wants to imitate. On the same hand Oyeku Kanran teaches us that self control, or *coolness*, brings admiration and respect. Violence is not a practical way to resolve conflict. All parties will surely lose whatever is most precious to them. Besides, the taste of the fight will stay long in the air. Fighting never produces wealth. When it seems to, it later produces shame which never goes away. Ifa tells us that fighting among Eniyan is not pleasing to Olodumare because people will always come to harm. Besides, it gives a bad name. It is a fearful state of mind that causes us to care not about the well being of our opponent who might even die during the fight. All involved can lose their Grace because of one another's bad thoughts. This is why Oyeku Kanran says:

> *Child of wealthy man pulls the hoe.*
> *Child of pawn pulls the broken hoe.*
> *Made divination for Oyeku*
> *who was told to make sacrifice and ritual*
> *so that Elekan might not be killed on his farm.*

*Failure to make sacrifice led to fighting and death.*
*Don't you see Oyeku who killed Elekan on his farm?*

*Omo Olowo ni fa oko*
*Omo Iwofa ni fa Eru'ko*
*Difa foyeku ti won ni*
*Ko tebo teru Koma ba pa Elekan soko*
*Ipin alaisebo, igba aiteru*
*Eyin o royeku to pelekan soko?*

At the time of creation the only man on Earth was called Ekan. Later, as people grew about him – and even more appeared from other places far and near – he was crowned Elekan, the king of Ekan. Elekan was a man truly blessed by Olodumare. He was a very high chief with lots of money. Elekan had servants, and wives and horses to ride. But soon there appeared a man called Oyeku. Oyeku had very little money, but he had a small farmland very near the land of Elekan of which he was very proud. Elekan, seeing that Oyeku had property of his own wondered if it was possible that anyone else could own land, too? He went to his Priests to ask why all of the land was not his.

Ifa asked the Priests to speak of Oyeku Pelekan (Oyeku Kanran). In this way Ifa told Elekan that Blessings come in many ways. Elekan was asked to make sacrifice in order to assure that the Blessing of *Longevity* would remain with him. He was also told not to yearn for the property of others. And most certainly, he must never be found fighting over any matter. But Elekan was an arrogant man. In fact he *loved* fighting, an activity at which he was an expert. In this way he often cheated the have-nots. Indeed, Elekan was not a nice man at all.

Now as it happened Oyeku also sought the advice of Priests to see how he could improve his lot. He was told that since he found great Satisfaction in his life that he should make sacrifice in order to prevent trouble that was coming from others. He was warned of violence and confusion. Oyeku was told to pray that someone does not die while on his land. Despite all of the words of the Ifa Priests, Oyeku left the house of Ifa with sadness. He felt that even with all of the wise words spoken by the Priests, somehow his question had not been answered. Dissatisfied with the advice he had been given, Oyeku did not make the sacrifice.

One day, the servants of Elekan invaded the land of Oyeku and began to plant yam in an area which Oyeku had already tilled. Oyeku soon saw them and challenged their presence. He ordered the servants of Elekan to go away. The servants laughed at Oyeku and began to fight him. The workers of Oyeku joined the fight as well. After a time, news of the fight reached Elekan. Many thought that since Elekan was a chief and an Elder, and because the farm truly belonged to Oyeku that Elekan would quickly settle the dispute. However, Elekan smiled as he went quickly to his armory and brought out his many weapons. He gathered together all of the members of his family as well as his bodyguards and vowed to give Oyeku a lesson.

When Elekan and his family and his bodyguards arrived at the battle site they distributed the weapons to Elekan's servants. But, as Elekan shouted instructions and rained curses on Oyeku, he suddenly grabbed his chest and fell to the ground. And there Elekan died.

Quickly the news of the fight spread around to all corners of the land. Everyone who heard carried the news to his neighbour: "Oyeku killed Elekan on the farm." Soon a mob of citizens captured Oyeku, tied him with a rope and took him to prison for killing Elekan.

And so it happened; In this way Elekan lost his life and Oyeku became prisoner. And it was there, in prison, that Oyeku remembered the words of his Priests:

*Child of the Weathly pulls the hoe.*
*Child of the pawn pulls the broken hoe.*
*Made divination for Oyeku*
*Who was told to offer sacrifice and make ritual*
*So that he would not kill Elekan on his farm.*
*Failure to offer sacrifice led to fighting and death.*
*Don't you see Oyeku*
*Who killed Elekan on his farm?!?*

*Omo Olowo ni fa Oko*
*Omo Iwofa ni fa Eru'ko Difa foyeku ti won ni*
*Ko tebo teru*

*Koma ba pelekan soko*
*Ipin alaisebo, igba aiteru*
*Eyin o royeku to pelekan soko?*

Okay so what have we learned? You can't just go through life beating people up! But some people do try it. That's why you find soldiers ruling countries and making every one else miserable. You can buy your way through life if you want to, but eventually the Eniyan will stand against you and they will win! In the end, those with Iwa Rere will rule the world. And they will rule with wisdom, compassion, love and great creativity. Justice will reign and Olodumare will dance in the heavens. Ademola puts it this way:

*It is Gratitude that guarantees Happiness. Gratitude breeds cooperation and cooperation is the food of a Successful society. Elekan was the first man to walk the Earth. Honor and*

*Respect was surely his. Oyeku was the first to own his own Land. The Blessing of Wealth began with them both. Why should such men suffer? Because each lacked Gratitude. They fought one another and each lost his Grace.*

Aboru Aboye.

# CHAPTER EIGHT

## OTURA OSE

### THE DAY OF THE OWNER

More than any other immoral act the lowest is stealing, it destroys a nation. Like a sore festering in an unknown place, stealing and corruption leads to suspicion and to insecurity. These are miseries that destroy the spirit. The loss of one's property or goods to an unknown thief leads to burning anger. The loss of what one has to someone you know, the one you see, leads to lack of confidence and to despair.

The thief himself is displeasing in the sight of Olodumare. It is the intention of Olodumare that the Eniyan will live together, work together, seek and gain knowledge and grow in spirit together. That we will share our Goodness and enjoy the benefits of our grace together. Ifa tells us that Olodumare has promised Eniyan the fruit of our labor. It is not good to frustrate the intentions of God. Stealing is an unkindness that makes one unworthy of living with others.

In the Odu called Otua Ose, Ifa tells us that we should never steal the property of others. We are told that stealing does not befit the dignity or character of Eniyan. If someone steals once, no matter how beautiful the material or the amount of wealth he might gain, the stain of being a thief is permanent. Once a thief, a thief forever, is the sentiment that dwells in the minds and hearts of people. But the ultimate victory will be for the victim. Our Oral Scripture assures us:

*"All the days are for thief but just one day is for the owner."*

May God not give us a stealing child; one who has the habit of stealing, no matter his protections; Ifa has warned that one day you will surely be caught.

**Otura Ose:**
*Otuase bent down.*
*He moved in a squatting position,*
*Made divination for Odikan the gangster*
*who wore a special cap*
*and everyday caused people's sadness.*

**Otura bere**
*Onko see see*
*Difa fun Odikan olori ole tin de aburo*
*Eyi to nfi jojumo Pa omo araiye lekun kiri.*

Nobody liked Odikan. Odikan was a thief who used deep medicines to protect himself from being caught. He so armed himself that nobody dared to resist or fight him. Though he bragged about his skill as a thief, somehow no one ever actually saw him carry anything, only his weapons. However, it was known that Odikan carried a special medicine with him. Whenever he saw something to steal, he merely coughed and vomited a small gourd from his stomach. The mysterious gourd was filled with medicine. All that Odikan had to do was to sprinkle the medicine on whatever he wanted to take and the property would disappear. He then swallowed the gourd and went away. Ah! Odikan! When he returned to his den Odikan would cough the medicine up again. After reciting a few incantations, the stolen property would appear from the small gourd.

Odikan was the master of other thieves and sometimes shared his secret methods with his apprentices. Odikan had been warned since he was a child not to steal. His parents warned him and even Ifa warned him. Yet he would not stop. Odikan claimed that stealing was more profitable than any business in the town. He stole and he stole until he became truly great in thievery. And that is not all; not only was Odikan a thief, but he was also greedy. His parents and his children lived in poverty. And for this he was also famous. In fact, Odikan loved his fame almost as much as the wealth he gained.

All of the townspeople came to fear Odikan. It was Odikan who made the people feel insecure. It was Odikan who frustrated them and made them feel that hard work was useless because Odikan would steal whatever they earned. Odikan was a bold thief. In fact, he became so bold that he would send messages in advance to those he intended to steal from.

One day Odikan asked the Ifa Priests what he should do with his wealth. His stolen posessions were crowding him out of his house. The diviners told him to offer sacrifice and to stop stealing. They also said that he should return the property of others to their owners. He was told that the special cap that he often wore should be given to Esu because it is Esu who knows those who offer sacrifice and heed the advice of Ifa. The Priests told Odikan that he should make sacrifice. But Odikan refused to give Esu even a plate of palm oil and he pronounced Orunmilla a "mere man, black in complexion"! He said that his cap was the medicine that protected him during his "operations" and that the

Priests wanted it so that he could be arrested. "Liars," he called them.

When Esu heard this he decided to teach Odikan a lesson. He disguised himself as a hunter and went to meet Odikan on the way. But first he put on a cap exactly like the one that Odikan wore. He then gathered all of the members of Odikan's gang together and tied them to a tree. When Odikan saw Esu he frowned at the cap that he wore. "What an insult!" he shouted. "You, a small rat, have the nerve to challenge me?!?"

Esu and OIdikan began to fight. But quickly Esu turned into a leopard and pounced on Odikan throwing him to the ground. Esu then dragged Odikan all over town shouting "This is the face of a thief, a thief, this is the face of a thief!"

All of the townspeople tied Odikan to a tree in order to burn him. But Esu said "No. Burn his house and his property. Scatter the members of his family, and send him away to wander the Earth forever. Everywhere he goes people will know that he is 'Odikan, the thief.' They will jeer and shout and women and children will throw stones at him. The people of the Earth will despise him and his family."

And so it is today. A thief is the most despised man or woman in a community. Don't destroy the society you live in. Don't be the enemy of your fellow man. Ifa has said you should never take that which is not yours. Odikan was released to wander the Earth forever. All the people of the town danced and rejoiced because finally, it was the day of the owner... they sang:

*Gang leader of all the thieves has been caught.*
*Our minds are now at rest.*
*Odikan was the leader*

*Of all thieves in this land.*
*The terrible gang leader has been caught.*
*Our minds will be at rest.*

**Song**
*OtuAse bent down.*
*He was the one who squatted low,*
*Made divination for Odikan the gangster,*
*Who wore a special cap,*
*Whose deeds caused people to weep.*
*The gang leader of thieves was caught.*
*Our minds are at rest.*
*Odikan, the gang leader of all thieves in this land was caught.*
*Our minds are at rest.*

**Orin**
*Otura bere*
*Onko see see*
*Difa fodikan olori ole tinde aburo*
*Eni to fi ojojumo pa omo araye lekun kiri*
*Owo ba olori ole asinmin*
*Owo ba olori ole nileyi*
*Owi ba olori ole asinmin.*

Let me say something before we leave this one. Not all thieves are people like Odikan who steal material things. Many thieves are those who abuse those who are dependent on them. Like the boss who forces peole to work overtime for nothing in order to increase his profit. Or the merchant who overcharges because people need what he has to sell. Our subject here is character. You can have the character of a thief but never be convicted in court. Careful O! Remember that Ifa and Merindillogun are the Word of Olodumare. The Odu has said that one day will surely be for the owner.
Aboru Aboye

# CHAPTER NINE

## IKA TUA

### **THE PROMISE**

In African society (Eniyan) there is an essential oath between men. That oath, or promise (Ibura), is that "In your absence, I will never violate your wife." The same oath exists between women. It is the nature of a person to be deeply offended when their wife or husband gives him or herself to, or is taken by, another. Because of this, the oath of marriage is law. Ika Otura is where Olodumare has said so, so that we all will know our own promise. It is only in this way that society can exist. And society is the order of Olodumare.

It is we who punish ourselves. It is not any devil or evil spirit. It is we who are unfair to one another. It is we who destroy our society. Betrayal destroys the fundamental institutions of mankind. It is familihood that makes society possible. Society is built on promises. Society is destroyed when promises are broken, when we offend one another's sensibilities by taking away our individual pride. Marriage is the fundamental institution of society. Even the town, the tribe, the nation takes its guide from the family. Law itself begins with familihood. There is no family without a promise. The promise of faithfulness; that a man or a woman will not give themselves to another.

Ikatua, also known as Ika Alaparo, offends the spirit and can kill. From Ikatua we derive this lesson:

*Agbekulori was the Ifa Priest of Agbegenige.*
*Agbegenige was the Ifa Priest of Orongaindekun.*
*Orongaindekun made divination for Olokunderin*
*On the day that all women were in Olokunderin's possession.*
*Cobra who makes its home by twining round itself.*
*Boa in a marshy area speaks freely*
*Made divination for Ore, the little girl.*
*A thorn in a lying position makes a poisonous mouth*
*Made divination for Latilu child of Egba at Akere.*
*The one who shall have pointed mouth*
*Because you pleased me, so l appear.*
*I'm not your husband.*
*Straight tree beautifies the forest,*
*Rainbow befits the heavens.*
*You who should desist from being flirty.*
*It was at the point of the road that we met.*
*I'm not your husband.*

Ore also looked backed at him and said:

*Slender stick befits the bush.*
*Rainbow befits the heavens.*
*You should desist from being flirty.*
*You, go with the burden.*

*Agbekuleri lawo Agbegenige,*
*Agbegenige lawo Orogaindekun,*
*Oronganindekun lo difa fun Olokunderin.*
*Lojo ti gbogbo obinrin rogbayika,*
*Oka lofi kika sele.*
*Ere logbe abata lahun*
*Difa fun Ore, omodebinrin okun*
*Ogan gbe ibule fenu soro*
*Difa fun Latilu omokunrin Egba Alake*
*Eyi ti yoofi sonso pari enu*

*Ore rire lore mi wa o*
*Emi kii soko re*
*Oju ona lagbe pade o*
*Emi kii soko re, igi tere ye igbo*
*Osumare ye oju Orun*
*Iwo ni awogi mAseju Ajaga lorun e*

Olokunderin was in want of a child. Though he had many wives, none of them had ever become pregnant. One day Olokunderin said that he had had enough of this and went to the Ifa Priests. The Priests told Olokunderin that a girl child would be born to one of his wives. The child would be called Ore. They said that the girl will bring with her an iwo (something bad and dangerous) which will be known to all by a special mark on her neck. They also said that if that child did not meet with a man who despite her iwo would have her, she too would never become the bearer of a child. Olokunderin said that he was in need of a child. They made sacrifice for Olokunderin and his wife gave birth to a child. They named the child Ore Omodebinrin Okun.

As time passed, Ore grew into womanhood and herself was in want of child. She went to the Ifa Priests who, on seeing the mark on her neck, told her to make sacrifice. They said that only if a man becomes affected by her iwo, would she ever give birth to a child. Ore made the sacrifice and waited.

There came a man from Egba Akere called Latilu who, despite his many wives, was famed for being adulterous. His wives and children were ashamed. Wherever he went Latilu left broken homes and banished wives behind him. The people of Egba Akere did not want their town to be destroyed. Because of this Latilu was sent to live in exile, wandering the countryside in shame. Wherever he went people became outraged when Latilu commited adultry with the women of the town. And so he was banned from one town after another. Time without number, Latilu had been warned by Ifa to desist from commiting adultry. But Latilu continued his ways anyhow. The Priests even warned him that if he did not change his ways that one day a strange woman would pass to him a deadly disease. But Latilu continued. And so, carrying his habit of adultery with him, Latilu continued to wander from one town after another, forever searching for a place to settle.

One day, Latilu appeared in the market of a strange town. There, busily selling beads was Ore. Latilu felt a stirring inside of him and began to eye Ore. Ore realized that Latilu had been gazing at her and smiled when Latilu expressed his wish to buy beads. Of course Ore refused to sell to him, knowing that beads were not Latilu's desire. After discussion Latilu finally told Ore of his intention to marry her! Ore was happy since she also needed someone to end her woe. They both agreed that Latilu should come to her house. On the morning that Latilu was to visit Ore in to her home, before he arrived Ore put on her woe and waited.

It was after their play of love that Ore escorted Latilu to the road. She looked once more at the woe on Latilu's neck and smiled. When Latilu returned home everyone noticed that his neck was becoming heavier and heavier, and he also became shorter and shorter. Secretly he began to chant a verse to Ore:

> *Agbekulori was the Ifa Priest of Agbegenige.*
> *Agbegenige was the Ifa Priest of Orongaindekun.*
> *Orongaindekun made divination for Olokunderin*
> *On the day that all women were in Olokunderin's possession.*

> *Cobra who makes its home by twining round itself.*
>
> *Boa in a marshy area speaks freely*
> *Made divination for Ore, the little girl.*
> *A thorn in a lying position makes a poisonous mouth*
> *Made divination for Latilu child of Egba at Akere.*
> *The one who shall have pointed mouth*
> *Because you pleased me, so I appear.*
> *I'm not your husband.*
> *Straight tree beautifies the forest,*
> *Rainbow befits the heavens.*
> *You who should desist from being flirty.*
> *It was at the point of the road that we met.*
> *I'm not your husband.*

Ore sat in her house rubbing her growing belly while chanting:

> *Slender stick befits the bush.*
> *Rainbow befits the heavens.*
> *You should desist from being flirty.*
> *You, go with the burden.*
>
> *Agbeku leri lawo Agbegenige.*
> *Agbegenige lawo Orogaindekun.*
> *Oronganindekun lo difa fun Olokunderin.*
> *Lojo ti gbogbo obinrin rogbayika.*
> *Oka lofi kika sele,*
> *Ere logbe abata lahun.*
> *Difa fun Ore, omodebinrin okun,*
> *Ogan gbe ibule fenu soro.*
> *Difa fun Latilu omokunrin egba alake,*
> *Eyi ti yoofi sonso pari enu*
> *Ore rire lore mi wa o*
> *Emi kii soko re*
> *Oju ona lagbe pade o,*

*Emi kii soko re, igi tere ye igbo.*
*Osumare ye oju Orun,*

*Iwo ni awogi maseju*
*Ajaga lorun e*

This was how Latilu suffered Ore's woe. Strife and suffering are the consequences of adultery. Ikatura forbids adultery; it is left to you, both male and female, to follow the way of Orisa.

*Wait a minute, wait a minute!* Doe this Ese Fa only speak of adultery? Okay, let's go back to Olokunderin. You remember, the guy with all of the wives who couldn't get over the fact that he was destined to have no children. Have we not acknowledged that the yearning for children justifies an unending quest? Who can blame Olokunderin who did all that he could to finally impregnate one young lady who in turn unleased misery and woe on the world? At what point do we accept our destiny and face what joy there is in our lives? And then there is the matter of the "Promise of marriage." In saying that adultery defies the law and expectation of Olodumare have we not said that "jealousy" and the behavior that springs from it is natural and excusable? Consider that carefully. How do we behave when we have been wronged? Now please don't take this as a suggestion that we take unfairness or misfortune or every injustice lieing down.

For many of us Iwa Rere can be a sensitive and subtle thing to even define no less to maintain in our behavior. Don't we say that "a hungry man is an angry man?" To be a human being is not a simple thing. We must think and pray that we are right in everything that we do. (Yes, *everything)*. We must not say that because it is human to think this way or behave that way that we can disrupt society in order to change our destiny. We must know that sometimes we will even get it wrong. So slowly o! Think well and listen to the advice of your Priests and wise Elders and especially your Ori who knows what is good for you, and maybe, just maybe you have a chance to get it right. It is our prayer that you read this on time.

Aboru Aboye

# CHAPTER TEN

## IKA IRETE

### **THE BLESSING OF YOUR HANDS**

You know, religion can be strange. You have heard the saying "God helps those who help themselves." So you look at yourself and you have nothing in your pocket and no means of livelihood. No friends no property, no skills. Nothing. So you forget about the pastor and go look for an Orisa priest. You know, somebody down to Earth who can tell you what to do. So Baba Lloyd tells you that the Orisa says you have Ire. You know, Blessings and Goodness. And you tell him "Great! I knew it all the time! But where?" And Baba Lloyd says "It is in your hands, your hands will bring blessings. Just bring a goat and some dried fish and you will see it. Baba Lloyd ever tell you that? "All of the time" you say?

So what's my point? I don't know. I just want to say I know how it is some times. I really do. But look, let's leave that for a minute and come back to it. Ademola wants to talk about the guy who doesn't have that problem and never did. He wants to talk about the Holy Odu Ika Irete.

To be "Born into wealth" is a blessing from Olodumare. It is an advantage that can help us to accomplish our life's mission and we should be thankful. However, though good fortune may be your legacy, you should never fail to make your own contribution to the well-being and betterment of mankind. It is the work of your own hands that reveals Iwa Rere. It is Ikarete that tells us that it is not inheritance, or the wealth of our fathers, that gives meaning to our lives. Rather, it is how we use the good fortune that we were born with. We should work hard to sustain our inheritance and bring honor to what we already have. Inheritance is a stepping stone. Your mother might have money, your father might have horses, but reliance on them can be your downfall. You see, you do not know the source of their wealth or how many people they owe. It is the work of your own hand that displays Iwa Rere and accomplishes your destiny so that you can help others to accomplish theres.

This is how Ikarete speaks of "Born into wealth (Inheritance)."

*Awuruku Sehinda*
*The road does not reject anybody.*
*The road does not reject bad people.*
*The road does not reject good people.*
*The road does not reject the one with the big head (dwarf)*
*Made divination for someone who relies on his parent's wealth.*
*But who will forever be in poverty.*

*People of Ipo, People of Offa (near and far)*
*Did you see the one who relied on his parents wealth*
*And found himself in deep poverty?*

*Awuruku Seyindenda*
*Ona ko ko eni kan.*
*Ona ko ko eni buruku.*
*Ona ko ko eni rere.*
*Ona ko ko Arara, Abori jinjin kunjin.*
*Adifa fun Agbojulogun*
*Ti o fi ara re fosita*

*Ero Ipo, Ero Ofa*
*Eyin O ri agboju Logun*
*To fi ara re fosita.*

Long ago there was a man blessed with property and wealth. He had hundreds of palm trees that were already fruiting. He had wives and workers and many, many children. But then one day one of his sons decided to change his name. Boldly the son gathered a band of drummers and chanters and ordered them to march through the town praising him like this:

> *Agbojulogun. (son of the wealthy man)*
> *He spends money like he mints it.*
> *He does not work.*
> *He says "after all I was born into wealth."*
>
> *Agbojulogun nawo bi eni tin ro*
> *Ko sise, ko sabo*
> *Oni owun kuku ma ri imiran lola.*

Many of his relatives were shocked and embarrassed. They called Agbojulogun into their council meetings and warned him to find his own work. "You are not the first to be born to a wealthy man," they said. But Ajogbulogun did not listen. Even his father instructed him to find something to do. Still Ajogbulogun did not listen. Instead, he built houses and married many wives.

One day the father of Ajogbulogun became ill and could no longer work. And then the truth came out. Though the Father of Ajogbulogun had many farms, he really owned no land at all. It was a long time ago that he had begged for the land, and because he was trusted as a hard and wise worker, his requests were always granted.

Over time he hired many workers and worked very hard and became successful. He always remembered to pay tribute to the landowners and they, too, were very happy.

Later, when this rich man fell into sickness, his entire family became confused because no one knew how to run the farms. Not knowing what to do, they all began to spend whatever money they could find. Many behaved as though the money would never run out; they went about boasting that they were now in charge and spent the money they found lavishly. When the money ran out they didn't mind, they merely began to sell his horses and stopped paying the rich man's workers. His barns fell into ruins and his crops were washed away.

After some time the rich man died. All of his relatives gathered together for his burial ceremony. All of his trusted workers came together to agree on what their master had instructed them to do in the event of his death. He had told them that all of the land should be returned to the owners and that his children should divide his real wealth among themselves. They did as they were told, but by that time there was little wealth left. Only the old man's clothes and his chieftaincy beads could be found while his house was falling into ruins.

And so the wives and the children shared the legacy as the old man had said, but the little that remained for Ajogbulogun was hardly a fortune. He wondered aloud, what would he do? Someone found a small bag of cowries under the old man's mat. Ajogbulogun's wives fought over it while their children cried and the townspeople laughed. "Look at them," they said, "disgracing themselves over their husband's pitiful inheritance. Ajobulogun...rich man indeed!"

And in this way Ajobologun found that though he had the legacy of a big man, in reality he had nothing.

Indeed, the actual legacy of the big man was not money at all. Rather, he left behind a tradition of hard work, honesty and integrity. But Ajobulogun had none of these. Neither had he any skill or talent. Ajobulogun did not even have credit to start his own farm. The landowners knew that he knew nothing of farming or managing men! The townspeople began to laugh at them saying that Ajogbulogun has become a poor man, what will his drummers shout?

Don't you see that we are each born to accomplish some small thing, big or small? Ajobulogun looked at his father's accomplishments as his own, and fell into poverty and disgrace. Praise Ikarete, may this never happen to you. May you learn to do something, and may you do well the things that you do.

Okay, that story is kind of pathetic wouldn't you say? But hold up a minute will you? Remember, you read with *Ire Owo*. The Blessing of your Hands. And if you listened to the Odu the truth of this is in Ademola's last sentence. "May you learn to do something, and may you do well the things that you do." So get the goat and the dried fish with your very last borrowed dime. Then ask Baba Lloyd to lend you some money to enroll in a course or to apprentice yourself to somebody. Then let the world see you trying, you know, displaying your Iwa Rere. And be surprised. Ire is something you have to pull. You work on your right and the Ire comes from your left. Your priest can tell you where it is. He really can. Believe me I'm not being religious, I'm being for real. Iwa Rere l'eso Eniyan.

Aboru Aboye

# CHAPTER ELEVEN

## OYEKU OSE (OYEKU POSE)

## **THIS LIFE IS A RIVER**

Oh boy, you still there? Well, maybe you'd better close your eyes and do some breathing exercises before you read this one because it is going to be deeper than deep. If Ifa is about Wisdom, you are about to get a serious dose. See you on the other side.

Don't you know that from death springs the eternal Grace of Olodumare? It is here, in Oyekupose, that Ifa tells us not to fear death. Feel free to wonder, is death even real? Is life not an ever flowing river that never returns but eternally refreshes itself? Death is the certain blessing which gbogbo (all) Eniyan receives with life. Death is the beginning of Renewal. Worry not and listen well as Ifa explains what you should plainly see.

Unbearable odors, sickness and pain, heartache and hurt, guilt and sorrow all end with death. But, so also does joy and happiness. Certainly if we do not die, the world will be covered by unbearable odors. The fruit of the Earth can never feed us all. It will be gobbled by the few and curses and cruelty and the noise of hatred will discolor our lives. Hunger will accompany illness and pain, and all manner of difficulties. Misery will forever be the lot of Eniyan.

Even the plants that surround us and flower our lives and nurture and feed us gradually, softly become dry. In peace we cut them and put them to fire. And soon, even from beneath their very ashes we see them again, appearing with goodness and hope just as before. For wisdom's sake, let us look to those who are tortured by unending pain and decay. If not for death, it is they who might writhe in agony forever. Death is relief. It is also the beginning of renewal, renewal which follows hope and happiness, joy and discovery and accomplishment and pride. It is only the carcass of this life that dies; later we return through our children. Others of us continue through the work that we have done, through the legacy that we leave behind. Death comes when the soul can no longer tolerate the body, and even struggles to leave. This is what we call "death." The soul has left the body. The body doesn't know when the ground covers its bad odor. In this way, we the living are left to take comfort that death is truly a Grace.

Oyekupose helps us to know that life is, in fact, a river. We go forward and we step backward; life stands forever. Ifa reveals to us the truth which our eyes cannot plainly see. That life is indeed unending and in truth, we never perish. In fear we will leave, but in joy we return. See how Oyekupose explains to us the Grace of death:

> *He who is happy will pray for long life (Awo ile alayo)*
> *If one suffers and lives long, misery is his lot (Awo ibanuje)*
> *If death comes we give thanks to Olodumare*
> *These were the great Priests of Ifa,*
> *Who went to divine about death in ancient times.*
> *"Why did Olodumare create death?" they asked.*
> *"Why is everyone born to die?"*

And Orunmilla answered, "Death is the blessing from God," Because stable water is slum water. Slum water is stinking water.

*Kama tete ku lawo ile alayo*
*aiteteku ise lawo ibanuje*
*Biku bade ka yin olorun logo lawo oloto*
*Awon lagbagba sanko-sanko*
*To lo difa iku wo lojo kini*
*Eese tiku n pani ti ko si eni ti kii ku?*
*Ojo na ni Orunmila so pe ore lolodumare fi iku se*
*Tori omi ti ko saan siwaju, saan seyin Lomi ogodo*
*Omi ogodo lomi egbin.*

It was on that day that Orunmilla revealed that "Death is a Divine Grace" (A gift of Olodumare). Water which does not flow becomes a pond. The pond is the home of filth.

*Water carries (Eniyan) this way.*
*Water carries (Eniyan) that way.*
*Let the sick return home*
*to receive another life (body)*

*Omi n gbewon lo rere*
*Omi n gbewon bo rere*
*Okurun karele*
*Lo re gba awo tuntun wale*

Oke Tase (The Mountain of Ase) is just to the east of the Garden of Peace (Ile Ife), it is the place to which Orunmilla descended from Heaven, and where three Great Elders appeared to greet Orunmilla, the Master of Fate. "Why does death kill"? was the question that troubled their hearts. "Death, that leaves no one untouched."

"Aya gbo, aya to o," (You have made ebo, you are Blessed) the Master of Fate greeted them in return. "But why this urgent inquiry about death?" he asked. "So that we do not die early!" The Elder of the three explained to Orunmilla that he had personally visited the Priest of the House of Joy. He had gone to pray for Happiness.

But it was there that Ifa told him that it was unwise to wish "never to die." Orunmilla laughed. "Is it because you are never in want of food and drink that you do not want to die?" The first Elder was puzzled. "Surely, whoever enjoys a full stomach will want to live forever." Orunmilla said.

The second of the three spoke next. "But I was smarter," he said. "I visited the Priest of the House of Sadness, to beg that I never meet death."

"But why such fear of death?" Orunmilla asked.

"Because death is misery" the second Elder answered. And what was the Priests reply?

"If one suffers and lives long, misery will surely be his lot," he said. Orunmilla told him that it was because he had not yet enjoyed his life that he feared death. Certainly, if he had the opportunity for enjoyment he would not want to die. For the eternally miserable who begs for food and drink, death is certainly a blessing, so why not give thanks to Olodumare? In all languages people say, "Where there is life there is hope." And then the third Great Elder spoke.

"I have known a man who saw death in his path," he said. "Unafraid, he came to bid his friends and honorable men 'farewell.' But where he went, I do not know." Orunmilla answered, "It is your very Honesty that leaves you unafraid, but you consider your knowledge to be incomplete. If you consider the things I have told you, you will know that death is the greatest Blessing of Olodumare."

The three wise men were grateful for the answers Orunmilla gave to them. But still they were not satisfied.

"Why did Olodumare create death?" they still wanted to know. It was then that Orunmilla took them to a beautiful flowing river from which he told the three Great Elders to drink and to cool themselves. The wise men did so.

Next Orunmilla took them to a river that was not flowing, one that gave off a stinking odor and was filled with larvae and insects and dirt. Once again Orunmilla told them to drink from the motionless river, but of course they refused. He then explained that the second river is called a "pond" which is the water of unpleasantness. "It is a fate worse than death," he said. He explained that the fresh river is the river of life that flows and empties itself never becoming a pond. And that one day it will flow freshly again, renewed and ever refreshing to those who encounter it. Life, like water, should flow with freshness and eventually surrender itself for renewal so that it can flow freshly again. Death is not the end of life; in many ways it is the beginning.

Nuff said, I say.

Aboru Aboye

# CHAPTER TWELVE

## IROSUN OGUNDA

## CHARACTER (IWA LEWA) MAKES A MAN

Okay, it's your turn. Let's go back one more time to the beginning. To the proverb that all children In Yorubaland learn, "Iwa rere l'aso eniyan." You remember, "Good character is the cloth that covers the Children of God." In other words, "good character" can be *seen* in the way we "carry ourselves." Even in the way that we walk and move, in fact in everything that we do. You say you got that? Our *personal* Iwa is shown when we display the essential values and ethics of our *culture* in our day-to-day lives.

But you know, when you think about it, having a predefined idea of what we should wear can be a problem. Being fashionable can be fun, but it can also be a pain. These days with culture changing and blending with the benefits and tastes of other cultures, where really does your culture begin and end? Who is it that determines our ethics and our tastes in an ever changing world? A world that we all want to belong to but still in our individual way. Even in Nigeria there is a popular saying "Who no like beta ting?" (You understood that right?) But the real questions becomes, *what is* "beta ting?" Isn't my bling beta ting? My Cadillac car? My fine fine bobo? Certainly the clothes that we wear to make ourselves feel good become more influenced by valuesand tastes that are, let us say, decidedly <u>not</u> of my culture…but dag! What about cultural change? Why not the global village because I ain't never seen no African village!?

But hold on. We are not suggesting what people should wear or how they should flow, but maybe, just maybe, it would be nice, or just best if we take a minute to define and redefine our changing tastes just to be sure that we are not being dragged along into a style or swag we really would not choose if we had choices. Maybe we should do a check to see if our Iwa is still rere, or if it has gone buruku. Buruku? So what is "buruku?" Well, let's just say that buruku means bad, and bad Iwa is Iwa Buruku. All over Nigeria, no matter what language you speak, when we do bad, stupid or inconsiderate things people call you Olori Buruku! In English that means you are the owner of a bad head. In Brooklyn it means "Man, you don lost yo mind!" So, let us see how one Odu of Ifa, Irosun Okunwa, cautions us to understand who we are, while reminding us that the cloth that we wear outside should intentionaly reflect the cloth that we wear inside.

This is Irosun Okunwa:

> *Dog is pleasant while its teeth are still white.*
> *Ram is pleasant while its beard is long.*
> *A dog does not have a beard.*
> *Let us find a ram to honor our ancestors*
> *Made divination for Head and for Character.*
> *When coming from Heaven to Earth*
> *It is Character that is most important.*
> *No Head is bad in the Kingdom of Ife (The entire world)*
> *It is Character that is most important.*

> *Aja sun won titi, Aja fi de eyin*

*Agbo sunwon tiroro, tiroro*
*Aja o ni roro ka rele lo re magbo wa*
*Ka fi bo Eegun ile baba eni*
*Adifa fori, abufun Iwa*
*Lojo ti won ntorun bo waiye*
*Iwa nikan loo soro*
*Ori kii buru kofi dale Ife*
*Iwa ni kan lo soro.*

To be clear, when we say that "no Head is bad in the Kingdom of Ife," we mean that God does not send stupid people to earth, which means that it is on coming to Earth that some of us just lose it. Lose what? Lose the ability to define who we are. Now it's not everybody that gets lost in trying to define themselves by applying what they see as "the style of the day." Some of us do remember who we are, or rather who we <u>were</u>, because basically that is who we are. It is on Earth that we forget that we are Children of the Kingdom of Ife all of whom have good heads. Here on earth? As opposed to what? Okay, let me get a little wild. Now I know most of you know nothing of the the music we call "The Blues." Blues is an old traditional music form that Black people used to talk about life. I remember a once popular song by a Chicago blues singer named Jimmy Reed. And it went like this.

*Bright light, big city, gone to my baby's head.*
*Whoa,*
*bright light, and big city, gone to my baby's head.*
*tried to tell the woman, But she don't believe a word I said.*

Now back in the day when they used to have Blues Week at the Apollo we thought that that song was funny. But it's only now that I realize that Jimmy Reed was like a Babalawo talking about our anxiousness to change who we are when we see something that excites us. Of course change is fun, we call it *fashion* and we use it to express ourselves, to creatively define our individuality in the language of an ever changing culture. Let us see how Irosun Okunwa recalls the path taken in our journey from Heaven to Earth and where we are going today:

At the command of Olodumare, before any one of us can come to Earth we must first select our Ori (inner head). And before Ori can come to Earth he or she must first choose our Character. We are each offered two choices. The Odu Irosun Okunwa tells of a time when Ori was asked to choose between "Good Character" and "Bad Character." Ori considered them both but he finally chose Good Character because it was both beautiful and wise both inside and out. He left Bad Character behind because it was incomplete and appeared to be faulty.

After choosing his Character Ori was instructed to move to the Crossroad between Heaven and Earth. There, Character became shadow (Ojiji) who would follow the new arrival on Earth wherever he went for the rest of his life. When Ori realized this he was pleased. He knew that Ojiji could never fade and would be his companion forever.

In the meanwhile, back in the Sky, Ori Ikeji (The younger brother of Ori) was also anxious to accompany a new arrival on Earth who wished for the best of life. Like his brother before him, Ori Ikej was asked to choose his Character. Ori Ikeji had seen that while Good Character had wisdom, and that wisdom led to wealth, he also learned that Bad Character knew how to use other people's money to acquire even more wealth.

"Come, take me and let us go" Bad Character said to Ori Ikeji."I will show you how to become a Billionaire!" Ori Ikeji hesitated but Bad Character then showed him a beautiful woman.

"That is another man's wife," Bad Character said. "But don't worry about that, she can be your happiness and together we will fight anyone who objects."

Ori Ikeji chose Bad Character and after stopping to pick up Ojiji, off they both went to live in the world.

When they were both in the world Ori of Good Character watched his younger brother Ori Ikeji as he planned and schemed to get all that he wanted in life. He saw with sorrow all of the sadness that the Bad Character he had chosen caused others. Soon Ori Ikeji was known to everyone as Olori Buruku; everyone despised Ori Ikeji and did what they could to avoid him. Gbogbo Eniyan (All of the Children of God) rejected Ori Ikeji for his Bad Character. Before long the Awon Atoni Aiye (The Mothers who Rule the Heavens) began to spread confusion and place traps in Ori Ikeji's path. Since he had disgraced himself and could make no progress on Earth, Ori Ikeji had to return to Olodumare. But, you know something? That wasn't the end of it. We have said that Iwa rere <u>covers</u> the children of The World. And what covers us can be changed…right?

So to his own surprise, when he arrived in The kingdom of Ife Ori Ikeji was told to go and choose his Character all over again, that there was still a chance for him to do well on Earth. This time, when he was offered Iwa Buruku, he threw it to the ground and chose Iwa Rere instead.

One day while Ori was bathing at the river Awinrinmogun, Ori Ikeji appeared in the bush. At first Ori didn't notice until he heard all of the townspeople who had gathered at the river praising Ori Ikeji for his Iwa Rere.

"You have done well," Ori told his brother. "Now, if you want to follow me you should do so for one hundred and sixteen days. In that time, with the help of Gbogbo Eniyan and Awon Atoni Aiye you will learn the ways of Goodness."

Ori Ikeji had learned that a bad head can be exchanged for a good head and having learned his lesson, this is what he did. Clearly Irosun Okunwa reminds us that as you were in The Kingdom of Ife, so should you forever be. Iwa Rere is your immortality.

Now there is this other blues song that goes……no never mind. Ifa is speaking, Perfect silence.

Aboru Aboye

# CHAPTER THIRTEEN

## OTUA IRETE

### **CHOOSING DESTINY**

Okay, so now we know all about choosing our destiny, picking up our Ori and coming to Earth right? But there is still another point that comes in the Sacred Odu Otua Rete. You see our personalities, our wisdom, our consciences, are all aspects of our Ori that are seen in our vert visible Iwa. Ori is who we are, including the person who originally came to earth from the Orun and at the same time it is our guide. The crazy thing is that important details of our lives are chosen even before we are born and according to criteria we will never again know or understand. But the bottom line is that <u>we chose</u> our own fortunes, be they good or bad, ourselves. Since Ori is the essence of who we are, it is we who even choose our parents! But what you want to know is why would anyone choose a bad Ori or knowingly come to Earth as an Olori Buiruku?

The sacred Odu Otua Rate tells us "Those who chose morning shall not die in the afternoon; and those who chose afternoon shall not die in the morning." So, what in the world does that mean?

Alright, let's look at it this way. What if, as we pass through life, we decide that we don't like the path that we have chosen? What if we have chosen poverty and now weep when we see our children in rags? What if we find ourselves lazy, and because of this we fail to accomplish anything because laziness is a flaw in our character? Well, Otua Rate also tells us that if we hold fast to our culture and our spiritual traditions, that is, if we pray and make sacrifice according to the divine scripture provided for us by Olodumare, if we do these things and then get up abnd beginb tyo walk the path that would liker to be known for, some of the choices that now displease us might be changed for good forever. In other words you don't have to return to the Kingdom of Ife in the literal sense. After all the Orisa are the distributors of Destiny. So through prayer, sacrifice <u>and hard work</u> we can sometimes cause that Destiny to change. You got that? Prayer, sacrifice and hard work. Or in Yoruba *Adura, ebo ati sise.* It is Orunmilla and all of the Irunmale (Orisa) who have the power and the authority to grant our prayers and accept our sacrifices. It is Ori who selects our destiny, and it is Ori who, in sharing our experience, can guide us in changing our fate. May the Orisa forever accept our praise and hear our appeals.

Okay if you got that, and you are ready to take off that awful dress, here is a story from Otua Rate.

> *The words of Ifa escaped the Priest until he saw calamity.*
> *The novice in Ifa knows no bad*
> *until it touches him.*
> *Read Ifa for Alukoso Aiye and Aludundun Orun*
> *"Keep listening" Alukoso Aiye,*
> *"Our destinies are not the same."*
> *Ogbon sa awo mawi*
> *Oro kan ologberi mamo*

> *Adifa fun Alukoso Aiye Abu fun Aludundun orun*
> *Alukoso Aiye, se ongbo*

*Ototo la yan eda o, ototo.*

Aludundun Orun (The Dundun[26] drummer of Heaven) and Alukoso Aiye, (The Koso[27] drummer of the Earth) were friends. They were knowledgeable and wise men who were often able to advise those whose Ori was bad. Each had been given a special duty which they attended to diligently. The Aludundun of Heaven was so called because he was placed at the crossroad between Heaven and Earth, a place that all travelers must pass on their journey to Earth. As each Ori appears, he or she is obliged to bow solemnly before the Aludundun in order to select their destiny. It is then that they announce what they intend to do on their journey through life. They even declare the time when they will return to Heaven.

By virtue of his assignment, it was not for the Aludundun Orun to utter a single word on hearing the chosen destinies of those travelling to Earth. His is only to add the authority of Olodumare to each person's .ronouncement by resounding it on his divine talking drum. And so, as each individual passes, the dundun speaks thus:

*"Let it be so, Authority comes from Olodumare".*

Thus there came a time when three extraordinary children appeared at the crossroad between Earth and Heaven. They said they were going to the Alukoso of the Earth whose duty it was to announce to one and all the arrival of any new person from Heaven.

The first of the three children dutifully stepped forth prostrating respectfully before the Aludundun of Heaven in order to choose his destiny. As he lay in the traditional position he said, "I am going to the Alukoso of Earth so that he will announce my arrival in the world of Eniyan." The Aludundun smiled. "But I will not spend more than three days in that place," The first child continued, "On the third day, when they set the fire for the mother of a new born baby, I will roll myself into it and thereby return immediately to Heaven." The Dundun drummer of Heaven was shocked at the first child's words. However, his sacred role was to beat his drum thusly:

*"Let it be so. Let it be. Let it be so. Authority comes from Olodumare"*

The second child to come was a woman who also brought her chosen destiny to be acknowledged by the Aludundun of Heaven. The woman also said that she was going to the Koso drummer of Earth who would then announce her arrival on his beautiful drum. She said that she would grow to be a very beautiful woman and would be very successful in her business. Because of this she would be loved by all. She then said that while on Earth she would not give birth to a child. Rather, during her marriage ceremony she would be offered a morsel of food. The food would contain a kind of pepper that would pass through her nose, and this would cause her to return to Heaven immediately. Remembering the words of the first child, the dundun drummer looked confused, but dutifully, he pronounced the woman's destiny with his holy drum.

The third person was a boy who said that when he got to the Earth he would be very popular and well loved by everyone. He also said that it would be a long while before he married, and that on the day of his wedding, as he took the traditional bath of the groom, a huge snake would appear and bite him. "At that precise moment I will return to Heaven," he said. Sadly, the Aludundun Orun drummed out the destiny of the third child.

Finally the three travelers from Heaven arrived at the gates of the Earth. There, according to tradition, the Alukoso Aiye asked the reason for their journey and the time of their return to Heaven. On hearing their answers he merely shrugged and announced their arrival.

It was on the third day following the arrival of the three extraordinary children from Heaven that the Alukoso received the news. The first of the travelers had been born to a young mother on the day of his arrival just as he had said. And on the third day, while his mother soundly slept, the new baby quietly rolled himself into the fire and died. Everyone blamed the mother for the child's death. They claimed that she always slept and slept, and now she had killed her own child by sleeping. Her husband left her and soon she was banished from the town. No one would ever hear of her again. On hearing the news the Alukoso Aiye of Earth was saddened and, remembering the announced destinies of the remaining two extraordinary children prayed to Olodumare to change the destinies of both.

Following the destinies that they had chosen in Heaven, both the second and the third children from Heaven lived to reach the age of marriage. But the Alukoso of the Earth, remembering the fate of the first child, still worried. Using his powers over the fate of those on Earth, he arranged their marriages for the same day; though the ceremonies would be done in different places, he would participate in both weddings as a drummer whose job it was to pray for the well being of the celebrants.

And so the Alukoso watched nervously as the senior sister was joyously carried to her husband's house at almost of the same time that the third child went to take his wedding bath. At the new home of the bride, amidst drumming and chanting, food was ceremoniously brought from the kitchen to welcome her. But it was not long before their joy turned to tears for as the very first morsel entered her mouth, she began to cough on a pepper which immediately entered her nose. In helpless desperation, all of the celebrants watched as the new wife choked on the strange pepper and died. As Alukoso passed the house, this time in silence, the second extraordinary child returned quietly to Heaven.

And what, you may ask, of the last child from Heaven who took his fated bath as the newly wed bride ate her meal of destiny? I am sure that you need no drummer to tell you that as he stepped into the shower stall, just behind his family house, an enormous snake suddenly bit him. Before anyone knew what had happened, the bridegroom too was dead. With great sorrow, the family and the bridal entourage of the departed new wife arrived at the house of the Koso drummer to tell of the ill fortune of the second child from Heaven. There they met the news of the husband-to-be who had been bitten by a big snake and died. They were surprised that the Alukoso already knew what had happened. Expressing his sadness he explained that "We all choose our own destiny before coming to Earth, and those of us left behind can only wonder."

With no other explanation he asked to be left alone to ponder what appeared to be unexplainable. As the crowd left the Alukoso quickly seized the time to travel to the crossroad between Heaven and Earth. "Were you not there when the three children chose their ill-begotten destinies?" he demanded of his friend, the Aludundun Orun.

"The word of Authority comes only from Olodumare" the dundun drummer explained to his brother. "My only role is to beat to the individual's request. While I might offer advice, I, like you, have no power to change what has already been chosen. If you wait and watch well," he continued, "you shall see many people passing from Heaven to Earth with intentions that wil truly make you wonder."

And so Alukoso watched in amazement as the Aludundun went about his work. Indeed, the crossroad between Heaven and Earth was a noisy place as the People of Heaven arrived to announce their destiny. Obas made the request that they be crowned as Obas, so also, Chiefs chose to be installed as chiefs. Those who wished to be crazy chose accordingly; while the child who only wanted to take a quick peek at the world before returning asked the Aludundun to "Please hold my sandals for me, I will be right back." He who wanted to live to an old age chose longevity.

Soon the Alukoso saw the first extraordinary child, the baby who rolled into his mother's fire, coming again. "I have come to re-choose my destiny," he said. On prostrating before the Aludundun, he continued, "I will return to the same mother, but this time I will wait a bit longer. However, when the time comes I will roll into the fire meant to keep me warm and return to Heaven."

The Alukoso was shocked and quickly placed his hand on the head of the drum pleading, "Please, you must hurry into the bush and cover your ears," he begged as the extraordinary child stared and, wondered who this strange man was, "you can watch but do not pronounce this sad destiny," The Alukosohe continued.

The Aludundun of Heaven looked at his brother with sympathy. "Please understand, I share your feelings" he said, "But I have my duties, and I must perform them."

Soon the second child, the man who was bitten by the snake on his wedding day, appeared and surely enough, he announced the same destiny as before. The Alukoso wanted to beg the man to change his mind, but the Aludundun stopped him.

Finally the Alukoso saw that the third child was also returning to the gates of Heaven on her way back to Earth. "I will not allow it!" the Alukoso shouted. Patiently, the Aludundun carried him back to his seat. "Perhaps these words will help you to understand. Lifting his drum the Aludundun Orun began to play":

**Song**
*Koso drummer of the Earth,*
*Indeed you must listen well.*
*Individually we choose destiny....individually.*
*Indeed, you must not forget,*
*Individually we choose destiny....individually.*

**Orin**
*Alukoso aiye songbo o*
*Ototo la n yan eda o ototo*
*Mase gbagbe o*
*Ototo la n yan eda o ototo*

Finally the last of the travelers to Earth had left. So also those returning to Heaven had all passed and the Aludundun of Heaven too sat down to rest. But the Alukoso of Earth was restless. "So many of these travelers have chosen destinies of doom," he said. "What can we do?"

It was then that the Dundun drummer of Heaven told his brother, the Koso drummer of Earth that, in fact, he was the one who could affect the destinies of travelers from Heaven. "Please, tell me how?" the Alukoso asked. "In fact, it is quite simple," the Aludundun said. "For example, in the instance of the child who is destined to roll into the fire, once the mother is fast asleep, simply place a banana lump in the middle of the fire. The child will roll herself into the middle of the banana which cannot burn. The child will scream and someone will rescue it before it comes to any harm. You, as a distributor of destiny (who just happened to passing by), will then announce on your drum that the child will live to an old age." The Alukoso smiled.

"Concerning the one who decided that pepper should pass though her nose," the dundun drummer continued, "she simply should not be allowed to eat on the day of her wedding; or if she must eat, she must not be allowed to eat the first morsel. You should disguise yourself as a drummer accompanying the bridal party and, by brushing against the bride at the proper moment, cause the first morsel to fall from her hand onto the floor. Of course it will then be thrown away and her chosen destiny will not be achieved." The Aludundun smiled, basking in his own wisdom. But the Alukoso was still puzzled. "But surely everyone must have a destiny!" he asked in confusion. "So you will then seal her new fate by boldly announcing on your drum that she too shall live to an old age." The Alukoso smiled proudly.

"And as for the man preparing for his marriage, he should not be allowed to take his bath. You should arrive early and ask your boys to clear the weeds around the bathroom and while doing so, kill the snake. To make extra sure, just before it is time for the husband-to-be to take his bath, you will first enter the bathroom to ease yourself (take a piss). You will pretend to be drunk, as drummers often are. On leaving, you will stumble badlyand knock over all of the barrels of water. The river is quite far and the man will have to take his bath elsewhere. In fact, he probably will not bathe at all. As everyone chastises and abuses you for your clumsiness, you will simply lift your drum and happily announce the man's new destiny of long life."

And so it happened. The Koso drummer returned to Earth and on the day the young wife gave birth to the first extraordinary child he quietly put a banana lump on the fire. When the child rolled into it and screamed, it was the Koso drummer himself who rescued the child and held it firmly in his hands. That is how death passed the child by.

As for the other two children who returned to Earth, as they grew, the Koso drummer watched them. On the day of the wedding of the girl, the new bride arrived at her husband's house crying for food to eat. But as the food was brought, the drummer knocked it from her hand to the floor. When the bride saw this she shouted in anger while abusing the drummer and insisting that she no longer wanted anything to eat.

On the wedding day of the soon to be married man, while carrying a pot of hot water to the bathroom, the Koso drummer drunkenly passed him, knocking the water from his hand and burning him. The bridegroom insisted that he could not bathe with cold water and so he got married without a bath. And that is how death also passed him by.

In this way Otua Rate tells us that individually we choose our destiny. But when we find that the path of our lives does reflect good character, do not be surprised if a friend, known or unknown, or of your Ori itself intervenes when it matters most. You should know that it is Olodumare who has the final say. Sometimes prayer and sacrifice can help us, sometimes it is Ori. If youdecided to be an armed robber when you were in Heaven, you can decide to be the blessings of long life and usefulness to your fellow man. And there is another thought. Can you of good character be the drummer for someone who has chosen badly?

> *Alukoso drummer of Earth,*
> *Indeed you must listen well.*
> *Individually we choose our destiny....individually.*
> *Indeed, you must not forget,*
> *Individually we choose our destiny....individually.*

> *Alukoso aiye songbo o*
> *Ototo la n yan eda o ototo*
> *Mase gbagbe o*
> *Ototo la n yan eda o ototo*

So what does "individually" mean? It means it is you who chooses the clothes that you wear. So, check yourself out and choose your destiny.....individually! And another thing, who is this Koso drummer who can spot your destiny and change it if he wishes? The next time you dance at an Orisa festival or bembe, see if you can spot him. Dance until he notices you and pray for his blessing. You know, Individualy. Hope you left something for Esu before you left the house. And again, you asked "why would someone choose a bad head in Heaven?" I'm not quite sure. Just stupid I guess.

Aboru Aboye.

# Chapter Fourteen

## OTURUPON MEJI (OLOGBON MEJI)

## THE TORTOISE AND THE SNAIL (IJAPA ATI IGBIN)

Now I know you've been waiting for this one. At last, a good old fashioned African folktale. So gather round the Iroko tree children (don't be scared now!) and listen up.

African people everywhere admire those around them with knowledge. Knowledge of the habits of animals bring success to hunters. Knowledge of the needs of plants and and the timing of the seasons guarantees the farmer a successful harvest. The knowledge of the blacksmith provides tools that help us all, and the knowledge of the midwife gets mother and child safely through the crisis of birth. So that's the place of *knowledge*. But what exactly is *Wisdom*?

Well wisdom is the proper understanding of one's knowledge placed in the context of life.

So what does that mean?

Well, put simply, wisdom is seen in the way we apply knowledge to our lives. We like to listen to certain people talk about life right? (Hopefully your parents or your Olorisa are included in that number). And that is why we welcome and treasure the presence of elders. But most of all, when you think about it, we gain our truest wisdom from our encounters with life itself, including our observations of the experiences of others. It's true, even the animals and things and places of nature are sources of wisdom. But some will say that the deepest wisdom and our understanding of life is gained through our *experience.*

These are teachings of Oturopon Meji, sometimes called Ologbon Meji, which in this simple verse tells us:

> *It is impossible for the Wiseman to know the amount of water in a rag.*
> *It is impossible for the Sweeper to know the amount of sand on the floor.*
> *No Traveler knows the end of all roads.*
> *Divined for Ijapa (Tortoise) who wished to tie the wisdom and power of the world to the limb of a tree.*
> *"Igpin (The Snail) is wiser than Tortoise," the people said,*

*Ologbon Aiye kole ta koko omi Seti Aso karibi mun*
*Moran mo ran kan komobi Ile gbe pekun*
*Adifa fun Ijapa to fe lore ko gbogbo ogbon aiye ro <u>Sori igi</u>.*
*Gbogbo ogbon ti Alabahun ba <u>gbon</u>*
*Eyin lo nto igbin.*

In the early days, Ijapa was so knowledgeable that no one was ever able to correct him. But people liked him, though they laughed at his claim to all of the knowledge in the world. Ha! Even when he misbehaved his explanations and excuses caused others to smile and forgive him. Indeed, Ijapa was respected by all. Despite his pompousness, everyone considered him to be a very smart and very brave man. Whenever there was any animosity they called on Ijapa for mediation. He even came to be called the "Father of Wisdom" because of his popularity, and all of the praise that was heaped on him.

But Ijapa soon grew proud, so proud that he came to believe that it was he and his family alone who should enjoy the knowledge that he possessed. There even came a time when he would not even speak to others, believing that his knowledge was too precious to be shared. "It is a secret," he would say with his nose in the air to those seeking advice or who asked him to explain various aspects of life.

One day, while passing through the market, Ijapa spotted a large gourd. "Aha," he said, "Just what I need!"

Happily Ijapa bought the gourd and immediately carried it to his house. When he arrived, he carefully carved a hole in the top. Then, opening it only slightly and looking around to be sure no one was watching or listening, he softly whispered into the hole all of his knowledge, carefully documenting all that he knew. "Where will I now hide this thing?" He asked himself. "Ah ha! I got it! How about that tall tree?"

When it was nearly dark, Ijapa set out with his gourd of knowledge. On reaching the foot of the tree he carefully placed a string around his neck and with it he hung the gourd on his chest so that he could take proper care of it. He then started climbing; but he quickly found that he couldn't climb very well because the gourd on his chest was in his way and he couldn't hold on to the tree. He tried and he tried but Ijapa still could not make it to the top of the tree. No matter how hard he tried, tortoise just kept falling back down to the ground.

Now as it happened, on the same evening that Ijapa decided to place his knowledge at the top of the tree, Igbin (Snail) was returning from his farm. As he moved slowly along, Igbin noticed Ijapa in his dismay.

For a long time Igbin just stood and watched Ijapa as he tried to climb the tree again and again, each time falling back down to the ground.

Finally Snail moved closer and called to Ijapa in a kind of snail whisper, "Hey, look, my friend, put the gourd on your back so you will be able to climb." Tortoise was surprised to hear these words of Wisdom from lowly, slow moving Snail. In fact, it had been a long time since *anyone* had given him any advice. After all he was Ijapa the knowledgeable. Right? But, even though he was reluctant to heed the advice of Igbin, Ijapa did swing the gourd around to his back and, while he was very tired from climbing and falling so many times, this time he climbed the tree with ease.

So there Ijapa was, at the top of the tree, looking down in wonder at the lowly, slow moving Igbin. Soon he started searching the gourd's contents to be sure that everything was there. Still noticing the Igbin looking up at him with a smile, he asked himself, "Why am I keeping this knowledge? If knowledge alone means wisdom, what about the stupidity I showed in tying the gourd to my chest?"

He looked down at Igbin again. Igbin smiled back, "Igbin is wiser than me," Ijapa said. Then, he sadly dropped the gourd to the ground and all of the knowledge melted into air. Suddenly, all of the people and all of the animals who had been watching from behind all of the trees in the forest appeared laughing and chattering away. "Igbin is wiser than Ijapa!" they said to one another, "Igbin is wiser than Ijapa!"

Anyhow, hope you liked the story. Now one more time, this is how the Babalawos tell it:

*It is impossible for the Wiseman to tie water in a rag.*
*It is impossible for the sweeper to know the amount of sand on the floor.*
*No traveler knows the end of all roads.*
*Divined for Ijapa who wished to tie the wisdom and power of the world to the limb of a tree.*
*"Igbin is wiser that Ijapa," the people said,*
*Wisdom is a gift to be shared*

*Ologbon Aiye kole ta koko omi S eti Aso karibi mun*
*Moran, moran ko komoye eepe Ile*
*Ari ona ka ko debi ile pe pekun Adifa fun Ijapa to fe lore*
*ko gbogbo ogbon aiye ro <u>Sori igi</u>.*
*Gbogbo ogbon ti Alabahun ba <u>gbon</u>*
*Eyin lo nto Igbin.*

Don't look at me, this is what the Babalawo said
But you know something? If I were you I would listen.

Aboru…..Oh, one more thing. Ssshhhhh.
    Ifa says that all Babalawos, and Olorisa, on leaving this mortal world arrive in a place called "Morere." Here Babalawo and Olorisa declare how they use the gift of Ase. If the Olorisa or Babalawo did not spread their wisdom, and utilize their given talent or Ase Orisa for the benefit of others, both the Babalawos and the Olorisa will be sent out of Morere never to see the dream called "Ahonnamejia," the teacher of Odu that amplifies your talent and knowledge to the point of Wisdom.
    These are teachings of Oturopon Meji, sometimes called Ologbon Meji.

Aboru Aboye.

# CHAPTER FIFTEEN

## IRENTEGBE

## TRADITION: THE SALVATION OF THE TOWN

W ho are we other than "those people who dress this way, or speak that way?" or who "observe this festival or that holiday?" Who are we other than "the people who came to this place from that place in search of this or that to be used for this or that in this or that way? The people whose virtues are these and whose skills are those?" Who are we if not "the people who worship Olodumare in this way or that way?" Who are we? Irentegbe says, "We should remember that we are who we are, or we become nobody."

Ifa warns us to hold fast to our ancestors' traditions regarding character, religion, language, our ways of livlihood and our customs and observations in order that our town does not perish. Those towns, those families with no religious tradition or observation, that lack language or custom, have perished. No one even remembers their names.

May Olodumare grant that we do not become a people without identity. In this way Irentegbe tells us to follow faithfully the tradition of our parents:

> *Flat stone, the Priest inside the water*
> *Who read Ifa for Oosanla Oseregbo*
> *When he was in want of a child.*
> *He had fasted without ceasing.*
> *Yet his wife carried no child on her back.*

*He offered sacrifice*
*So that he could have the blessing of a child.*
*Soon Oosanla Oseregbo gave birth to Irin (fish trap)*
*He gave birth to Ebiti (rat trap). Finally, he gave birth to Iwodere (fish hook).*
*After giving birth to these children*
*Oosanla became sick and could not stand up.*
*He was asked to offer six fish as sacrifice.*

*Ota pete Awo Abe Omi*
*Oun lo difa fun Oosanla Oseregbo*
*To nfomi oju seraun omo*
*Onfara gba awe airipon*
*Won ni ko rubo, orubo*
*Won ni ko teru, oteru*
*Nitori ati le bimo*

*Kope ko ijina, igba Oosanla sebo*
*Obi Irin, obi ebiti*
*Obi Iwo dere ti somo*
*Ikeyin wori lenje lenje*
*Leyin to bi awon omo wonyi*
*Oosanla wa nsogbo gbo Arun*
*Onaju ati dide*
*Won ni koru eja mefa lebo*

It was when Oosa (You remember Oosanla Oseregbo? Well Oosa is short for him) became sick, so very sick that he remembered what always works. He said to the Pastor and to the Imam and to the dokita too (wherever they came from) each of who sought to help him, that *fasting* was not the tradition of his elders; that *sacrifice* was the tradition. So when Oosa prepared to give sacrifice, he sent Irin, the Elder son, to go and catch fish.

But stupid Irin, he did not ask of his own sacrifice. He did not follow tradition. When Irin got to the river, rather than lowering his trap to the bottom of the river, he lowered his head inside the water! Can you imagine? Something he had never done before. He did this a second time. The third time Irin entered the water, his string broke and Irin sank to the bottom of the river.

Oosanla waited and waited. He worried for his son whom he could no longer see. Not knowing what else to do, Oosanla sent Ebiti to find his brother Irin. Though Ebiti was in no way wise in the ways of the river, he also failed to follow tradition by asking his Ifa Priest what might befall him in the land of the fish. Instead he depended on his knowledge of the *Earth*. He thought he was smart. In order to enter the water, Ebiti made legs of mud. Can you imagine? He, too, has never been heard from again.

    Oosanla was worried. Would he ever see his sons again? What should he do? One day he decided to send Iwodere, the youngest of them, to look for his two brothers. But even though, very unlike his brothers, Iwodere was wise in the ways of the river, he had carefully watched the ways of his father and decided to inform his Ori of his intended venture. Iwodere visited his Ifa Priests so that he would return safely from the river. It was Irentegbe that assured him that he had done well:

    **Song**
    *The things of which they were born were never of their taste.*

*He who prefers the culture of others*
*Were the Priests who read Ifa for Iwodere*
*Who walks intimately with fish.*

*The wealth I am looking for, that my hands cannot reach*
*Iwodere Ifa should give it to me*

**Orin**
*Ohun abi won bi ki wu wun*
*Ti eni eleni ni ya won lara*
*Adifa fun Iwodere,*
*ti o salabarin eja*
*Ire ti mo wa ti owo mi o to*
*Iwodere Ifa ni o fa fun mi*

Would Iwodere find his brothers? Would he catch fish for his father? These were the reason for his divination. The Priests told Iwodere that he would not perish if he brought as sacrifice things of value on Earth and put them into the river as offerings. Iwodere offered the river things of the Earth.

On arriving at the river, the people of the river told Iwodere that when his brothers Irin and Ebiti were advised to offer the fish things that were of value to them on Earth, that the brothers told the fish that they should be content with what their parents have left for them. That they should shun the belongings of others. But fish ignored the suggestion. What was already in the water was there in abundance. The things of the Earth were what they expected of the stranger. Neither Irin nor Ebiti were ever heard from again. The things of the Earth that Iwodere brought with him as offerings brought happiness to the fish. Surely enough, the fish began to eat the things that Iwodere held in his hands. In this way they found themselves on land, and that is how they were caught.

Oosanla used the fish for sacrifice, and it was then that he was relieved of his illness. Those on dry land whoenter the water, not knowing the ways of fish, will surely perish. Let us appreciate that which is ours. Let us value those things that are traditional to us. Let us offer what we have to others and receive honor and wealth in return. Oosanla was sad at the loss of his two sons. But he praised Iwodere for his wisdom, his faith and his high regard for his own traditions. Oosanla, even in his grief, remembered to dance for Iwodere and to be joyous. He said "All of the Goodness that I have longed for has been brought to me by lwodere."

Irentegbe says that we should always let those things that belong to us be to our liking. And, to be careful of other people's belongings. Surely, it is the town that abandons it's own traditions to follow the ways of another that will be lost forever.

Aboru Aboye

# Chapter Sixteen

## OYEKU MEJI

### A WORLD WITHOUT ELDERS

Now what could be the meaning of that? "A world without elders?" Without experience? A world without wisdom? Only the scratching and groping and whining of children? Ah! But of course. Ifa has chosen this Odu to warn us against tyranny. At least we hope so. If not that....WHAT?!?

Okay. Okay. Don't panic, but let's not be stupid either. Oyeku Meji clearly tells us that 'Elders should never cease to be on Earth and that our youth should never say that "an Elders' mouth is stinking." Now don't look at me, that's how the Babalawos put it. Thay have told us to "Walk near them because they cannot mislead us. Let the smallest child move with Elders," These are the instructions of Ifa, so that "we will understand the meaning of 'good character.' Okay good, Iwa Rere again.

We are told to "take good care of our Elders in order to gain their favor." Why? "Because they are closer to Olodumare than we. We need their gentle words for our advantage." How does Oyeku Meji tell us this? Well, by now you know there is a story. In ancient times the words of Ifa were a bit, shall we say, strange but, if you are ready, be patient and gain a final bit of wisdom in a crazy story:

*The dried mud wall will scatter when it falls.*

*The moist mud wall becomes a solid foundation*
*Cast Ifa for the people of Ode Apa*
*Who asked how they should kill their old people.*

*The dried mud wall will scatter when it falls.*
*The moist mud wall becomes a solid foundation*
*Made divination for a young boy*
*Who refused to kill the old people.*
*He who knows fish will become the Alapa of Apa.*
*Praise be to Alapa who knows fish.*

*Puu, Ogulutu*
*Isu Iro bale ro po*
*Difa fun won lode Apa*
*Won ni ki won o pa Arugbo ile won.*

*Puu, Ogulutu Isu Iro bale ro po*
*Difa fomo to ko ti*
*Ko parugbe ile re*
*Eni mo eja kasai wa je*
*Alapa Alapa oma ku omo Eja.*

Okay, Okay, fish huh? If you are still there let's take a look at this. It only stands to reason: "If you kill off your Elders, how will you know the things you must know in order to survive?"

*Kill off our Elders?* O pari! Why do we keep repeating the obvious?

But Ssshhh now! Ifa is speaking...perfect silence! Remember that the purpose of scripture is to tell us of times beyond memory, of times unimaginable. Indeed, the Holy Odu Oyeku Meji speaks of a time when the young people of the city of Apa complained that their old people were too harsh, they were the problem, they were even corrupt. To harsh? So harsh that they killed them?

Yes...killed them! Okay, I've said it. Now listen. The young people of Apa complained that the Elders of their town gave them no peace. One day they asked, "Would it not be better if we did not see any old people at all?" For this reason the young people of Apa conspired to kill all of their Elders.

> Shut up now! Yes, the young people of Apa conspired to kill all of their Elders. Now listen to this story.

Only then, they reasoned, would they have peace.

> Please, you must not run away; I promise there is something to be learned here. Go on Ademola.

And so all, well, let us say <u>most</u> of the Elders of Apa were killed. Yes, children murdered their parents. That is all of them.... except one, and here begins the lesson.

> You remember the Young Boy in the poem above. If you don't remember, go back and read it again.

Now there was this boy who <u>did</u> listen to his Priests who instructed him that his Elders held the keys to his success and also that it was not proper to kill anyone, especially one's parents.

> *"Mmm Hmmm, geniuses."*

> Look, I heard that, don't you be fresh with me! Respect the Babalawo.

And so the Young Boy kept his father and his mother together on the farm. He knew well that his parents who trained him and brought him up should now be taken care of. That it was proper and he wanted to do it. He also remembered the words of Ifa that said 'the day his mother died would be the day his gold broke, for indeed his mother was his gold.' And that the day his father died would be the day that his looking glass fell into the water. Because only through his father would he ever see his own path through life.'

> *Now that is the Ifa that we all know! Can we go now?*

> Will you ever shut up!?

Now the Young Boy, believing the words of his Priests, went deep into the farmland of his father and built a hut. And there he kept his old people. At night he prepared food to his mother's taste....

> *Now even I would like to have been there for that!*

....and slept beside his father on his mat.

Each day the Young Boy appeared in the town and no one suspected that his parents were alive and carefully cared for on his farm. But listen well, this is only the beginning. You think it is amazing that the young people of a town would kill off their Elders so that they could have peace? Hmmm. Well what if we told you that fish suddenly began falling from the sky?

> *Ha, ha, ha, I was waiting for that one. See you another time. Aboru....*

> Look, Ademola, with respect, please don't make this harder than it already is. And you sit down!

One day it began to rain. And months later it seemed that the rain would never stop. It rained and rained and rained. At a point it rained so much that fish, yes fish began to fall from the sky.

> Wait, come back! Does Ifa lie? Does Ifa jest? Hey, forget them Ademola. Look, I'm still here, continue please.

Even the youth of Apa who watched their homes wash away and the crops of their farms turn to mud asked aloud, "What kind of 'thing' is this? Could it be that God himself is angry that we have killed off all of our Elders?" Many of them were certain that the fish that appeard in the storm were the souls of their Elders returning to Earth. Were they? Oyeku Meji tells us that it happened this way.

> *Okay, We are back.*

> Why?

> *Well I don't know how you did it but it's raining outside.*

> Okay. So sit down and shut up.

> *So what happened next?*

> I said shut up!.....OK. I'm sorry for shouting.

Now, certainly the storm was only the latest consequence of the massacre of the elders by the youth of Apa. Since that time they had never been able to agree on anything.

The entire society had fallen apart. Distrust ruled the land. Shame, fear. Gradually they came to realize that only the wisdom and the instruction of Elders can keep a town from rotting. And truly Apa had begun to stink. When the heads of families die the house becomes dilapidated, unless they are replaced by suceedingelders. Of which there were none.

And so they were left to wonder. "Who knows the meaning of these *things* that now drop from the sky? Anyone who knows shall be our king," the question itself was absurd. After all who was there to whom they could listen? Who was there to know? And then they remembered. Someone recalled the Young Boy who when ordered to kill his parents seemed not to agree. When they thought about it they realized that while his parents were no longer seen, no one had actually seen their bodies and that they had only assumed that he had killed them as the others had done. And so it was to him they now turned. This child who was different confessed that he had kept his own old people alive on his father's farm; that obedience and sacrifice had been his salvation; that his elders were well. He told them of the Odu Oyeku Meji,

The Young Boy's father had told him that those 'things' that were dropping from the sky were food meant for them all, but that with no advice, and in their fear, the others would shun them and starve. The father had instructed his son to find a special pepper and to cook them so that he might be able to share the food with his family. The child feared that his father wanted to kill himself and begged him to forgive the foolish young people of the town of Apa. His father told him not to fear while taking the soup made by the Young Boy.

On the third day Young Boy's father asked his son to prepare more of the soup made with the special pepper and to add more of the 'things' that had fallen from the sky. The father told the Young Boy that that which had fallen from the sky was called eja (*fish*). That it had originated in places called odo (*rivers*.) That eja had been carried by the storm from rivers to far away places and had fallen in their town as a blessing. "This soup is fine soup," he said. It is not the wrath of God, it is the joy of God.

And so this is what the Young Boy told the young people of Apa who had killed their Elders. One by one they feasted on eja. One by one they came to understand the curse that they had brought upon themselves. They kept their promise and crowned the Young Boy as their king with the title Alapamoja. The boy told them that he was grateful, but that anybody who made medicine and did not have the prayer of their father had not made medicine, but only soup. Elders cannot all disappear from the Earth. He told them that while everyone else had killed their parents, he had not. That his wisdom came from the teachings of his father. Many still did not believe him until the Young Boy's father appeared at his crowning. In celebration they gave him the title Baba Oba (Father of The King). Even the king has a father whose counsel to the Oba must always be followed.

Oyeku Meji teaches us to move with our Elders, to accept their guidance, and surely we will find the light and the good life. May Elders never die on Earth.

*So tell us Baba Lloyd, did Baba Ademola have to go through all of that just to say that we should honor, learn from and respect our elders?*

Would you kindly shut up!?

Aboru Aboye

# Afterword

Okay, if you've stopped laughing, let us review the purpose and the central lesson of **IWA RERE: Morality in Yoruba Traditional Religion**. We should remember that the foregoing are not *the* sixteen verses of Ifa that explain what is moral and what is not. True, each story, or Ese Ifa was selected from an Oracle (Oral Scripture) that contains the Sacred Word of God, as revealed over time to the Yoruba people of West Africa. What we should realize is that the Ifa Oracle is *African in nature* and as such there are no lists, just lessons that one by one reflect values that everyone is expected, and even *obliged*, to understand and follow whether they are versed in the Oracle or not.

African culture insists that each of us basically knows the rules and expects us to display moral conduct in our behavior and our attitude toward life and our natural surroundings in what we have called our Iwa.

Since most of us have grown up in a world in which the overwhelming influence of other cultures colors our expectation of where and how "rules" are *taught*, we thought a better appreciation of how recitations of Ese Ifa or Apataki Merindillogun convey African values of character in everything that we do would be helpful. Again, the purpose of telling these stories is to encourage us all to *think* Iwa Rere as we move through life and the world working together to build, maintain and secure a cohesive and healthy society while fulfilling the expectations of Olodumare, the Orisa and Egun.

Surely the Orisa will assist us as we struggle to bring peace, progress, security and well being to our families and the larger community that we are born to nurture, defend and to serve.

Ire O!


Lloyd Weaver
Ademola Fabunmi

# End Notes

[1] *Iwa Pele*, Good or exemplary character

[2] *Iwa Pele and Iwa Rere* are complimentary terms that recognize a person's good character. They are interchangeable terms for the same principle. Because it is the most commly heard in Nigeria, Iwa Rere is used as the title and the subject subject of this book

[3] *Orisa* are divine aspects of Olodumare (God) that are living and divine philosophical principles that are manifest in everything from phenomena of nature to human personalities. They are at once parts of and all of Olodumare. That are personified in thousands of stories of their adventures on Earth that provide lessons and instruction to guide the activities of adherents of Yoruba traditional Religion.

[4] *Olorisa* are men and women fully initiated into Yoruba Traditional Religion. While devoutly worshipping all Orisa each Olorisa is specifically devoted to one single Orisa. In some places all Olorisa are considered to be priests.

[5] *Babalawo*s are a special cast of priests who are devoted to an Orisa called Orunmilla. Babalawos are the keepers of Ifa, an oral scripture that many oinsidered to be the Word of Olodumare (God) and the basis for Yoruba traditional Religion. The primary function of Babalawos is to commit Ifa to memory and to constantly recite its chapters (Odu), verses (Omo Odu), stories (Ese Ifa) and songs (Orin) and more for the benefit of mankind.

[6] *Odu* refers to the Sixteen basic Chapters of the Ifa and Merindillogun Oral Scriptures.

[7] *Two hundred and fifty-six commandments.* Here Ademola refers to the two hundred and fifty six Omo Odu, or verses, contained in the sixteen Chapters of the scripture called Ifa. Among other items of sacred knowledge aqnd inspiration, each Omo Odu contains a specific lesson concerning morality.

[8] *Aseda of Ijo Orunmilla in Lagos.* Major groups of Babalawos in many Yoruba towns or cities are organized under the leadership of the *Araba* who heads a house of Ifa chiefs. Some will say that the Araba answers only to the Oba. Others will say that he is the *equivalent* of the Oba. The second in rank in the circle of Babalawos is the *Aseda*. The title is derived from the first witness or student of Orunmilla.

[9] *Godson.* During the period of the Atlantic trade in human beings, captive hundreds, perhaps thousands of Olorisa and Babalawos found themselves in different parts of the Americas. As they secretly organized themselves into small religious bodies they substituted the language of their captors and as a means of survival. Senior Olorisa, who in Africa would have called their initiates and apprentices "awo" or "omo", adapted the convenient Christian terms in Spanish, French and Portuguese in order to hide their relationship. Though this is rapidly changing, English speaking Olorisa, particularly in North America, still commonly refer to initiating priests and their initiates as their Godfather/Godmother who refer to them as Godchild. Some say that these deliberate retentions are in remembrance of the brave acts of their ancestors who faithfully practiced their religion through centuries of severe repression..

[10] *Eniyan* refers to "mankind." In the Yoruba undersanding the family of man is one single body that emanated from the original creation of humanity at Ile Ife. Therefoe the nations of the world are the Ife diaspora. Creation, particularly when it coimes to human beings is ascribed to Obatala who is often praised as rthe Creator God, or God of Creation or even the father of Orisa. Obatala is the epitomy of Iwa Rere. However the creation of humanity was also accompanied by the complications of humanity. In the stories found in Ifa, (which often contradict one another), Oduduwa is seen to have usurped the role and the glory of Obatala by defeating him militarily and ensconcing himself on the throne of Ife and becoming known as the Father oif Mankind who dispersed his children to form the nations of the world. Indeed much of the unity and pride of Yorubas is expressed in their common reference to themselves as Omo Oduduwa.

[11] *Ebo.* One of the definitive aspects of Yoruba religious tradition is the opportunity to change destiny through ritualistic prayer and sacrifice. In this instance prescribed objects from nature that reflect the conflict in our lives and the character of of the Odu are offered to an obliging Orisa. Symbolic offerings range from inanimate objects such as fruit or other foods or leaves to animals whose habits reflect the philosophical or spiritual principle referenced by the Odu.

[12] *Merindillogun.* While Ifa is the scripture that is read, recited and interpreted exclusively by Babalawos whose lives are devoted to its impeccable preservation, every Orisa, as an aspect of Olodumare, also has access to the sacred word. While Ifa is "read" by means of the manipulation and casting of sixteen palm nuts which are the personificatioin of Ifa, an art at which the Babalawo is adept, each of the other four hundred and one Orisa and their priests access the Word of Olodumare, and also themselves divine through the systematic casting of sixteen cowerie shells. This scripture or oracle is known as Merindillogun.

[13] OBGBESE. Each of the sixteen Odu has a name. Within each Odu there are 16 chapters known as Omo Odu which are combinations of the Primary Odu. The present Omo Odu is a combination of Eji Ogbe and Ose. In a kind of slang it is referred to as Ogbese. Every Omo Odu has one or more slang references and these are used throughout this book. Sometimes more than one will be used within an explanatory discussion or within the Ese Fa itself. This is how it happens in real life so we will exercise that privilege here. In other words we will not explain this every time.

[14] *Olodumare.* Simply put, God, the Creator, Maker of All Things, Maker and Guiding Force of the Universe and all that we will never imagine. Yoruba Religious Tradition is a monogamous spiritual concept. This is not said for purposes of aligning it with other monogamous religions, but simply because it is true. Similar to other religions Olodumare eminates in different aspects or persons. These "Divinities" are called Orisa. Each Orisa is a person of God. Olodumare has at least one hundred other names that are basically descriptions of the undescribable. In additionto Olodumare the most common are Olorun (Owner of The Sky) and Olofin Owner of the Palace).

[15] *E wura O!* ("Good morning" in archaic Yoruba; E pele ("Softly" or "sorry", a common very polite greeting that acknowledges that one might be disturbing the one being greeted); Aje O (" Money O!"A parting wish to a passing hawker or polite wish to someone selling.)

[16] *Esu.* Esu/Elegbara is the antithesis of Orunmilla. If Orunmilla is the Orisa of destiny, assuming that what will be will be, Esu is the Orisa of change, personifying the principle of spontiaity, allowing for even we human beings to imagine and invent what would otherwise never be. Perhaps it is in recognition of Esu that elders have been heard to say "Even Olodumare changes His mind." Esu is the Orisa that many fear because while he is surety, he is also unsurety. As we begin major undertakings we offer Esu/Elegbara the tidbits he loves the most. In doing this Obatala entered the market with a degree of certainty.

[17] *O pari!* This is the end!

[18] *O ma se!* What a terrible thing!

[19] *Odidere* Known outside of Africa for its grey plumage and bright red tail feathers as wll as the ability to talk, the African Grey Parrot (Called loro in Spanish) is the sacred bird of the Yoruiba people; its red tail feathers that adorn the crowns of Kings and Priests are often given as offerings to the Orisa.

[20] *Olofin.* We have said before that Olofin is one of the titles for God. It is not unusual for God to be personified in an Ese Fa alongside mortals or other Orisa. But, since Olofin means "Owner of the Palace", it is also occassionaly the title of a King. However since Obatala is the highest of the Orisa, the King of his town can only be Olofin (God).

[21] *Ire.* Blessings. In the Divine Oracles spefic kinds or sources of Ire are specified. The sources range from Olodumare him (or her) self, or from any or all Orisa or from one's Ori or one's ancestors or one's parents or ones children, or one's character and on and on. In is book Ire is also refereed to as "Grace," or "Goodness" or "Good things."

[22] *Time.* Since Olodumare is the Master of all things, He does not live His experience out in time. For him the past, the present and the future all exist together. It is we human beings who have to live out our experience in time.

[23] *Ase* refers to a Divine power or ability conferred on Priests or Kings or other initated persons that enables then to do specific

things. The Priest has the Ase to interpret Ifa or Merindillogun, or to call Orisa to accept sacrifice or to speak for Orisa. In this case, poetically, Ire has the Ase to confer specific Good Things on specific people for the betterment of their lives.

[24] *Iroko* is an Orisa that is the repository of the medicines of life and death. It keeps them for safety and for dispensation when the Odu commands and the ebos are performed. But Iroko is as arbitrary as life itself. Iroko resides in a specific tree that is the place for supplication and the dispensation of Ire. Because it is a tee, Iroko is the subject of awe and caution.

[26] *Dundu.n* An hour glass shaped drum with heads at each end that is carried by a strap that is slung over the shoulder. The drum is beaten with a curved stick. Leather strings are tightly stretched along the length of the drum so that when squeezed the tone if the drum changes. In this way tones and rhythms produce a language. Also known as gangan or the talking drum, dundun is used to celebrate occasions with praises and messages that most Yorubas understand.

[27] *Koso Drummer.* Koso is a quarter of Oyo that is devoted to the rituals of the Orisa Sango. Sango's special drum is the bata which when played replicates the cracking sound of thunder. So the "Koso drummer" is a bata drummer. Bata is played at the most sacred Orisa ceremonies and contains an Orisa itself called *Ayan* in Oyo Yoruba abd Anya in the dialect of the Lucumi where it's drummers are intiated as Priests. In Africa are chosen by virtue of their family lineage.

www.ingramcontent.com/pod-product-compliance
Lightning Source LLC
Chambersburg PA
CBHW050646160426
43194CB00010B/1835